Apemen

Separating fact from fiction

W9-AXD-380

DID HUMANS REALLY EVOLVE FROM APE-LIKE CREATURES? • WHAT
ABOUT THE SIMILARITY BETWEEN HUMAN AND CHIMP DNA? • THE
NEANDERTHAL • IDA: THE MISSING LINK? • MEET ARDI

A POCKET GUIDE TO . . .

Apemen

Separating fact from fiction

answersingenesis

Petersburg, Kentucky, USA

Third printing July 2011

ISBN: 1-60092-300-3

Printed in China

www.answersingenesis.org

Table of Contents

Introduction

People are fascinated with their origins. However, that fascination leads people down two different roads. Some start with an understanding that humans find their origin in an unidentified apelike creature that lived many millions of years ago. Ultimately, those who accept this interpretation of the past trace their lineage to a single-celled organism that allegedly lived billions of years ago.

The fossil evidence used to develop the explanation of human evolution has been found lacking in several ways. Despite the lack of agreement on the order of human progression, the general idea is accepted and the details remain to be worked out. Despite intentional frauds and constant reshuffling, our ape ancestry is proclaimed in arenas from the covers of magazines to the teaching in classrooms.

The Bible gives a distinctly different view. Man is not an ape that has evolved over time, but a special creation of God—made in the very image of God. The origin of different people groups is understood from the account of the events surrounding the Tower of Babel and the value of human life is based on the value given by the Creator.

Does what you believe about origins influence the way you view those around you? Should chimps be given the same status as humans? The Bible gives us guidance in answering these questions and many others.

Did Humans Really Evolve from Ape-like Creatures?

by David Menton

Television documentaries on human evolution abound. Some of the more popular in recent years have been *Walking with Cavemen* (2003) produced by BBC and aired on the Discovery Channel, *The Journey of Man: A Genetic Odyssey* (2003), produced by National Geographic and *Survivor: The Mystery of Us* (2005), also by National Geographic. All of these shows present as fact the story of human evolution from apelike creatures over the past several million years. They claim that anthropologists have found links in the human evolutionary chain and that scientists have "proven" evolution happens through DNA and other studies. But what is the real evidence for human evolution? What evidence are we not hearing? In this chapter, we will examine how anthropologists either make a man out of a monkey or make monkeys out of men. And once again, we'll conclude that the evidence points to the fact that man is a unique creation, made in the image of God.

Perhaps the most bitter pill to swallow for any Christian who attempts to "make peace" with Darwin is the presumed ape ancestry of man. Even many Christians who uncritically accept evolution as "God's way of creating" try to somehow elevate the origin of man, or at least his soul, above that of the beasts. Evolutionists attempt to soften the blow by assuring us that man didn't exactly evolve from apes (tailless monkeys) but rather from *apelike creatures*. This is mere semantics, however, as many of the presumed apelike ancestors of man are apes and have scientific names, which include the word *pithecus* (derived from the Greek meaning "ape"). The much-touted "human ancestor" commonly known as "Lucy," for example, has the scientific name *Australopithecus afarensis* (meaning "southern ape from the Afar triangle of Ethiopia"). But what does the Bible say about the origin of man, and what exactly is the scientific evidence that evolutionists claim for our ape ancestry?

Biblical starting assumptions

God tells us that on the same day He made all animals that walk on the earth (the sixth day), He created man separately in His own image with the intent that man would have dominion over every other living thing on Earth (Genesis 1:26-28). From this it is clear that there is no animal that is man's equal, and certainly none his ancestor.

Thus when God paraded the animals by Adam for him to name, He observed that "for Adam there was not found an help meet for him" (Genesis 2:20). Jesus confirmed this uniqueness of men and women when He declared that marriage is to be between a man and a woman because "from the beginning of the creation God made them male and female" (Mark 10:6). This leaves no room for prehumans or for billions of years of cosmic evolution prior to man's appearance on the earth. Adam chose the very name "Eve" for his wife because he recognized that she would be "the mother of all living" (Genesis 3:20). The Apostle Paul stated clearly that man is not an animal: "All flesh is not the same flesh: but there is one kind of flesh of men, another flesh of beasts, another of fishes, and another of birds" (1 Corinthians 15:39).

Evolutionary starting assumptions

While Bible-believing Christians begin with the assumption that God's Word is true and that man's ancestry goes back only to a fully human Adam and Eve, evolutionists begin with the assumption that man has, in fact, evolved from apes. No paleoanthropologists (those who study the fossil evidence for man's origin) would dare to seriously raise the question, "Did man evolve from apes?" The only permissible question is "From which apes did man evolve?"

Since evolutionists generally do not believe that man evolved from any ape that is now living, they look to fossils of humans and apes to provide them with their desired evidence. Specifically, they look for any anatomical feature that looks "intermediate" (between that of apes and man). Fossil apes having such features are declared to be ancestral to man (or at least collateral relatives) and are called *hominids*. Living apes, on the other hand, are not considered to be hominids, but rather are called *hominoids* because they are only similar to humans but did not evolve into them. Nonetheless, evolutionists are willing to accept mere similarities between the fossilized bones of extinct apes and the bones of living men as "proof" of our ape ancestry.

What is the evidence for human evolution?

Though many similarities may be cited between living apes and humans, the only historical evidence that could support the ape ancestry of man must come from fossils. Unfortunately, the fossil record of man and apes is very sparse. Approximately 95% of all known fossils are marine invertebrates, about 4.7% are algae and plants, about 0.2% are insects and other invertebrates and only about 0.1% are vertebrates (animals with bones). Finally, only the smallest imaginable fraction of vertebrate fossils consists of primates (humans, apes, monkeys and lemurs).

Because of the rarity of fossil hominids, even many of those who specialize in the evolution of man have never actually seen an original hominid fossil, and far fewer have ever had the opportunity to handle or study one. Most scientific papers on human evolution are based on casts of original specimens (or even on published photos, measurements and descriptions of them). Access to original fossil hominids is strictly limited by those who discovered them and is often confined to a few favored evolutionists who agree with the discoverers' interpretation of the fossil.

Since there is much more prestige in finding an ancestor of man than an ancestor of living apes (or worse yet, merely an extinct ape), there is immense pressure on paleoanthropologists to declare almost any ape fossil to be a "hominid." As a result, the living apes have pretty much been left to find their own ancestors.

Many students in our schools are taught human evolution (often in the social studies class!) by teachers having little knowledge of human anatomy, to say nothing of ape anatomy. But it is useless to consider the fossil evidence for the evolution of man from apes without first understanding the basic anatomical and functional differences between human and ape skeletons.

Jaws and teeth

Because of their relative hardness, teeth and jaw fragments are the most frequently found primate fossils. Thus, much of the evidence for the ape ancestry of man is based on similarities of teeth and jaws.

In contrast to man, apes tend to have incisor and canine teeth that are relatively larger than their molars. Ape teeth usually have thin enamel (the hardest surface layer of the tooth), while humans generally have thicker enamel. Finally, the jaws tend to be more U-shaped in apes and more parabolic in man.

The problem in declaring a fossil ape to be a human ancestor (i.e., a hominid) on the basis of certain humanlike features of the teeth is that some living apes have these same features and they are not considered to be ancestors of man. Some species of modern baboons, for example, have relatively small canines and incisors and relatively large molars. While most apes do have thin enamel, some apes such as the orangutans have relatively thick enamel. Clearly, teeth tell us more about an animal's diet and feeding habits than its supposed evolution. Nonetheless, thick enamel is one of the most commonly cited criteria for declaring an ape fossil to be a hominid.

Artistic imagination has been used to illustrate entire "apemen" from nothing more than a single tooth. In the early 1920s, the "apeman" *Hesperopithecus* (which consisted of a single tooth) was pictured in the *London Illustrated News* complete with the tooth's wife, children, domestic animals, and cave! Experts used this tooth, known as "Nebraska man," as proof for human evolution during the Scopes trial in 1925. In 1927 parts of the skeleton were discovered together with the teeth, and Nebraska man was found to really be an extinct peccary (wild pig)!

Skulls

Skulls are perhaps the most interesting primate fossils because they house the brain and give us an opportunity, with the help of imaginative artists, to look our presumed ancestors in the face. The human skull is easily distinguished from all living apes, though there are, of course, similarities.

The vault of the skull is large in humans because of their relatively large brain compared to apes. Even so, the size of the normal adult human brain varies over nearly a threefold range. These differences in size in the human brain do not correlate with intelligence. Adult apes have brains that are generally smaller than even the smallest of adult human brains and, of course, are not even remotely comparable in intelligence.

Perhaps the best way to distinguish an ape skull from a human skull is to examine it from a side view. From this perspective, the face of the human is nearly vertical, while that of the ape slopes forward from its upper face to its chin.

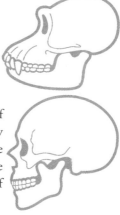

From a side view, the bony socket of the eye (the orbit) of an ape is obscured by its broad flat upper face. Humans, on the other hand, have a more curved upper face and forehead, clearly revealing the orbit of the eye from a side view.

Leg bones

The most eagerly sought-after evidence in fossil hominids is any anatomical feature that might suggest *bipedality* (the ability to walk on two legs). Since humans walk on two legs, any evidence of bipedality in fossil apes is considered by evolutionists to be compelling evidence for human ancestry. But we should bear in mind that the way an ape walks on two legs is entirely different from the way man walks on two legs. The distinctive human gait requires the complex integration of many skeletal and muscular features in our hips, legs and feet. Thus, evolutionists closely examine the hipbones (*pelvis*), thighbones (*femur*), leg bones (*tibia* and *fibula*) and foot bones of fossil apes in an effort to detect any anatomical features that might suggest bipedality.

Evolutionists are particularly interested in the angle at which the femur and the tibia meet at the knee (called the *carrying angle*). Humans are able to keep their weight over their feet while walking because their femurs converge toward the knees, forming a carrying angle of approximately 9 degrees with the tibia (in other words, we're sort of knock-kneed). In contrast, chimps and gorillas have widely separated straight legs with a carrying angle of essentially 0 degrees. These animals manage to keep their weight over their feet when walking by swinging their body from side to side in the familiar "ape walk."

Evolutionists assume that fossil apes with a high carrying angle (humanlike) were bipedal and thus evolving into man. Certain australopithecines (an apelike creature) are considered to have walked like us and thus to be our ancestors largely because they had a high carrying angle. But high carrying angles are not confined to humans—they are also found on some modern apes that walk gracefully on tree limbs and only clumsily on the ground.

Living apes with a high carrying angle (values comparable to man) include such apes as the orangutan and spider monkey—both adept tree climbers and capable of only an apelike bipedal gait on the ground. The point is that there are living tree-dwelling apes and monkeys with some of the same anatomical features that evolutionists consider to be definitive evidence for bipedality, yet none of these animals walks like man and no one suggests they are our ancestors or descendants.

Foot bones

The human foot is unique and not even close to the appearance or function of the ape foot. The big toe of the human foot is in line with the foot and does not jut out to the side like apes. Human toe bones are relatively straight rather than curved and grasping like ape toes.

While walking, the heel of the human foot first hits the ground, then the weight distribution spreads from the heel along the outer margin of the foot up to the base of the little toe. From the little toe it spreads inward across the base of the toes and finally pushes off from the big toe. No ape has a foot or push-off like that of a human; and thus, no ape is capable of walking with our distinctive human stride, or of making human footprints.

Hipbones

The pelvis (hipbones) plays a critically important role in walking, and the characteristic human gait requires a pelvis that is distinctly different from that of the apes. Indeed, one only has to examine the pelvis to determine if an ape has the ability to walk like a man.

The part of the hipbones that we can feel just under our belt is called the iliac blade. Viewed from above, these blades are curved forward like the handles of a steering yolk on an airplane. The iliac blades of the ape, in contrast, project straight out to the side like the handlebars of a scooter. It is simply not possible to walk like a human with an apelike pelvis. On this feature alone one can easily distinguish apes from humans.

Only three ways to make an "apeman"

Knowing from Scripture that God didn't create any apemen, there are only three ways for the evolutionist to create one.

1. Combine ape fossil bones with human fossil bones and declare the two to be one individual—a real "apeman."

2. Emphasize certain humanlike qualities of fossilized ape bones, and with imagination upgrade apes to be more humanlike.

3. Emphasize certain apelike qualities of fossilized human bones, and with imagination downgrade humans to be more apelike.

These three approaches account for *all* of the attempts by evolutionists to fill the unbridgeable gap between apes and men with fossil apemen.

Combining men and apes

The most famous example of an apeman proven to be a combination of ape and human bones is Piltdown man. In 1912, Charles Dawson, a medical doctor and an amateur paleontologist, discovered a mandible (lower jawbone) and part of a skull in a gravel pit near Piltdown, England. The jawbone was apelike but had teeth that showed wear similar to the human pattern. The skull, on the other hand, was very humanlike. These two specimens were combined to form what was called "Dawn man," which was calculated to be 500,000 years old.

The whole thing turned out to be an elaborate hoax. The skull was indeed human (about 500 years old), while the jaw was that of a modern female orangutan whose teeth had been obviously filed to crudely resemble the human wear pattern. Indeed, the long ape canine tooth was filed down so far that it exposed the pulp chamber, which was then filled in to hide the mischief. It would seem that any competent scientist examining this tooth would have concluded that it was either a hoax or the world's first root canal! The success of this hoax for over 50 years, in spite of the careful scrutiny of the best authorities in the world, led the human evolutionist Sir Solly Zuckerman to declare: "It is doubtful if there is any science at all in the search for man's fossil ancestry."[1]

Making man out of apes

Many apemen are merely apes that evolutionists have attempted to upscale to fill the gap between apes and men. These include all the australopithecines, as well as a host of other extinct apes such as *Ardipithecus, Orrorin, Sahelanthropus,* and *Kenyanthropus.* All have obviously ape skulls, ape pelvises and ape hands and feet. Nevertheless, australopithecines (especially *Australopithecus afarensis*) are often portrayed as having hands and feet identical to modern man, a ramrod-straight, upright posture and a human gait.

The best-known specimen of *A. afarensis* is the fossil commonly known as "Lucy." A life-like mannequin of "Lucy" in the *Living World* exhibit at the St. Louis Zoo shows a hairy humanlike female body with human hands and feet but with an obviously apelike head. The three-foot-tall Lucy stands erect in a deeply pensive pose with her right forefinger curled under her chin, her eyes gazing off into the distance as if she were contemplating the mind of Newton.

Few visitors are aware that this is a gross misrepresentation of what is known about the fossil ape *Australopithecus afarensis*. These apes are known to be long-armed knuckle-walkers with locking wrists. Both the hands and feet of this creature are clearly apelike. Paleoanthropologists Jack Stern and Randall Sussman[2] have reported that the hands of this species are "surprisingly similar to hands found in the small end of the pygmy chimpanzee-common chimpanzee range." They report that the feet, like the hands, are "long, curved and heavily muscled" much like those of living tree-dwelling primates. The authors conclude that no living primate has such hands and feet "for any purpose other than to meet the demands of full or part-time arboreal (tree-dwelling) life."

Despite evidence to the contrary, evolutionists and museums continue to portray Lucy (*A. afarensis*) with virtually human feet (though some are finally showing the hands with long curved fingers).

Making apes out of man

In an effort to fill the gap between apes and men, certain fossil *men* have been declared to be "apelike" and thus, ancestral to at least "modern" man. You might say this latter effort seeks to make a "monkey" out of man. Human fossils that are claimed to be "apemen" are generally classified under the genus *Homo* (meaning "self"). These include *Homo erectus, Homo heidelbergensis,* and *Homo neanderthalensis.*

The best-known human fossils are of Cro-Magnon man (whose marvelous paintings are found on the walls of caves in France) and Neanderthal man. Both are clearly human and have long been classified as *Homo sapiens*. In recent years, however, Neanderthal man has been downgraded to a different species—*Homo neanderthalensis*.

Neanderthal man was first discovered in 1856 by workmen digging in a limestone cave in the Neander valley near Dusseldorf, Germany. The fossil bones were examined by an anatomist (professor Schaafhausen) who concluded that they were human.

At first, not much attention was given to these finds, but with the publication of Darwin's *Origin of Species* in 1859, the search began for the imagined "apelike ancestors" of man. Darwinians argued that Neanderthal man was an apelike creature, while many critical of Darwin (like the great anatomist Rudolph Virchow) argued that Neanderthals were human in every respect, though some appeared to be suffering from rickets or arthritis.

Over 300 Neanderthal specimens have now been found scattered throughout most of the world, including Belgium, China, Central and North Africa, Iraq, the Czech republic, Hungary, Greece, northwestern Europe, and the Middle East. This race of men was characterized by prominent eyebrow ridges (like modern Australian Aborigines), a low forehead, a long narrow skull, a protruding upper jaw and a strong lower jaw with a short chin. They were deep-chested, large-boned individuals with a powerful build. It should be emphasized, however, that none of these features fall outside the range of normal human anatomy. Interestingly, the brain size (based on cranial capacity) of Neanderthal man was actually *larger* than average for that of modern man, though this is rarely emphasized.

Most of the misconceptions about Neanderthal man resulted from the claims of the Frenchman Marcelin Boule who, in 1908, studied two Neanderthal skeletons that were found in France

---

(LeMoustier and La Chapelle-aux-Saints). Boule declared Neanderthal men to be anatomically and intellectually inferior brutes who were more closely related to apes than humans. He asserted that they had a slumped posture, a "monkey-like" arrangement of certain spinal vertebrae and even claimed that their feet were of a "grasping type" (like those of gorillas and chimpanzees). Boule concluded that Neanderthal man could not have walked erectly, but rather must have walked in a clumsy fashion. These highly biased and inaccurate views prevailed and were even expanded by many other evolutionists up to the mid-1950s.

In 1957, the anatomists William Straus and A. J. Cave examined one of the French Neanderthals (La Chapelle-aux-Saints) and determined that the individual suffered from severe arthritis (as suggested by Virchow nearly 100 years earlier), which had affected the vertebrae and bent the posture. The jaw also had been affected. These observations are consistent with the Ice Age climate in which Neanderthals had lived. They may well have sought shelter in caves and this, together with poor diet and lack of sunlight, could easily have lead to diseases that affect the bones, such as rickets.

In addition to anatomical evidence, there is a growing body of cultural evidence for the fully human status of Neanderthals. They buried their dead and had elaborate funeral customs that included arranging the body and covering it with flowers. They made a variety of stone tools and worked with skins and leather. A wood flute was recently discovered among Neanderthal remains. There is even evidence that suggests that he engaged in medical care. Some Neanderthal specimens show evidence of survival to old age despite numerous wounds, broken bones, blindness and disease. This suggests that these individuals were cared for and nurtured by others who showed human compassion.

Still, efforts continue to be made to somehow dehumanize Neanderthal man. Many evolutionists now even insist that Neanderthal man is not even directly related to modern man because of some differences in a small fragment of DNA! There is, in fact, nothing about Neanderthals that is in any way inferior to modern man. One of the world's foremost authorities on Neanderthal man, Erik Trinkaus, concludes: "Detailed comparisons of Neanderthal skeletal remains with those of modern humans have shown that there is nothing in Neanderthal anatomy that conclusively indicates locomotor, manipulative, intellectual or linguistic abilities inferior to those of modern humans."[3]

Conclusion

Why then are there continued efforts to make apes out of man and man out of apes? In one of the most remarkably frank and candid assessments of the whole subject and methodology of paleoanthropology, Dr. David Pilbeam (a distinguished professor of anthropology) suggested the following:

> Perhaps generations of students of human evolution, including myself, have been flailing about in the dark; that our data base is too sparse, too slippery, for it to be able to mold our theories. Rather the theories are more statements about us and ideology than about the past. Paleoanthropology reveals more about how humans view themselves than it does about how humans came about. But that is heresy.[4]

Oh, that these heretical words were printed as a warning on every textbook, magazine, newspaper article and statue that presumes to deal with the bestial origin of man!

No, we are not descended from apes. Rather, God created man as the crown of His creation on Day Six. We are a special creation of God, made in His image, to bring Him glory. What a revolution this truth would make, if our evolutionized culture truly understood it!

1.   S. Zuckerman, *Beyond the Ivory Tower* (London: Weidenfeld & Nicolson, 1970), p. 64.

2.   *American Journal of Physical Anthropology* 60 (1983): 279–317.

3.   *Natural History* 87 (1978): 10.

4.   *American Scientist* 66 (1978): 379.

David Menton received his PhD in Cell Biology from Brown University. Now retired, Dr. Menton served as a biomedical research technician at Mayo Clinic and then as an associate professor of anatomy at Washington University School of Medicine (St. Louis) for more than 30 years. He was a consulting editor in histology for Stedman's Medical Dictionary, and has received numerous awards for his teaching. Dr. Menton is a popular speaker for Answers in Genesis and has spoken throughout the US and Canada on the creation/evolution issue for nearly twenty years.

Human Beings: The Fossil Evidence

by Gary Parker

What about ourselves? What can we infer from the evidence regarding the origin of human beings? Evolutionists now give us two choices.[1] Either human beings are the result of time, chance, and a ceaseless struggle for survival, or else we began as "a hopeful monster whose star was a bit more benevolent than most." According to creationists, the evidence suggests, instead, that we are here by the plan, purpose, and special creative acts of God.

I've mentioned being part of a television program on creation-evolution produced by the secular Canadian Broadcasting Corporation (CBC).[2] The program opened with a medieval princess wandering in a castle garden, apparently looking for something. Then the camera panned over to a rock ledge around a pond. There it was, big bulging eyes and all: a frog. Right before our incredulous eyes, the princess leaned over and kissed the frog. Stars sparkled across the TV screen, then a handsome prince appeared. As the prince and princess embraced, the narrator stepped into the scene with this introduction: If you believe a frog turns into a prince instantly, that's a fairy tale; if you believe a frog turns into a prince in 300 million years, that's evolution.

When I believed and taught evolution, I would not have put it that way, or course. But as I look back, I realize *that* story reflects what I really was teaching. According to evolution, if you simply wait long enough, time, chance, and struggle (mutation and selection) will gradually turn some amphibians, like that frog, into reptiles, mammals, apes, and finally man, like that prince.

Scientists can understand how a "machine" with as many complex and interdependent parts as a human being could be put together by intelligent creative design. Could chance and struggle over vast amounts of time do the same thing without any outside help and no planning ahead? Nothing in our scientific experience suggests time and chance have that kind of creative ability, although much of our common experience demonstrates that time and chance can *destroy* design! To convince scientists and skeptics, then, clearly the *burden of proof lies with the evolutionist* to find a series of fossils suggesting the change from frog to prince, or at least ape to man.

The first fossils proposed as links between apes and mankind were the "cave men" called Neanderthals. Neanderthal was originally portrayed as a "beetle-browed, barrel-chested, bow-legged brute" (a suitable ancestor for a mugger, if nothing else!) The creationists in those days responded, "Hey, wait a minute. Neanderthals are just plain people, some of whom suffered bone diseases." The first Neanderthals discovered came from harsh inland environments in Europe, where they could easily have (like many of our own American-plains Indians) suffered skeletal abnormalities, especially from lack of iodine in the diet and shortage of sun-induced vitamin D necessary for calcium absorption during the long winters.

Neanderthals from the Palestine area do not show the more stooped and massive features. The brain volume of Neanderthals is slightly *larger* than the average brain volume of people today, and Neanderthal peoples had a well-developed culture, art, and religion. Nowadays, evolutionists agree completely with creationists: Neanderthals were just plain people, no more different from people living today than one living nation is different from another. What were the "cave men"? Just people who lived in caves. (And at today's housing prices, that may once again be a good idea!)

There's a secular museum in Germany where the curator dressed the wax model of a Neanderthal Man in a business suit and tie. His reason? He said it was time to quit deceiving the public. Neanderthals were just plain people. Indeed, scientists now classify Neanderthals as *Homo sapiens*, the same scientific name given to you and me.

Tragically, Neanderthals have not been the only people once considered subhuman "missing links." In an article reprinted in *Natural History* as part of an issue on the history of evolutionary thought, there's a short but very sad article by Henry Fairfield Osborn.[3] Osborn says that a hypothetical unbiased zoologist from Mars would classify people into several distinct genera and many species. Thus, said Osborn, Negroes would be classified as a separate species, not yet evolved to full human stature. "The standard of intelligence of the average adult Negro," wrote Osborn as a so-called fact of evolution, "is similar to that of the eleven-year-old youth of the species *Homo sapiens* [which, for Osborn, meant Caucasians only]." Osborn was a leading evolutionist of the 1920's, and it is easy to see how his kind of evolutionary thinking (rejected by modern evolutionists) helped to pave the way for Hitler's Nazi racism in the '30s and '40s. (See also Gould, on the false science of "craniometry" and its terrible applications.)[4]

The Australian Aborigines were also once treated as subhuman evolutionary links. The natives of Tasmania were deliberately slaughtered by settlers who justified themselves by saying it was okay to kill wild dogs as farm pests, so why not other non-humans? As her dying wish, the last surviving Tasmanian, Truganini, asked that she be buried with her "people," not embalmed as a museum specimen. She died, was embalmed, and preserved as an evolutionary link. (Warning: few Christians stood against this horror, perhaps because many churches had already accepted evolution into their thinking.)

In 1912, speculation about man's ancestry shifted to Piltdown Man, dignified by the scientific name *Eoanthropus dawsoni*. Almost everyone knows that Piltdown Man turned out to be a deliberate hoax. But Piltdown Man wasn't shown to be a hoax until the 1950s. For over 40 years, the subtle message of the textbooks was clear: you can believe in creation if you want to, but the facts are all on the side of evolution. The *facts*, in this case, turned out to be a bit of ape jaw and human skull stained to make them look older.

One mystery is who perpetrated the Piltdown hoax, but the real mystery is *why did anyone believe it?* It was *not* a particularly clever hoax. As Gould[5] points out, when people looked at the teeth with the right hypothesis in mind, "the evidences of artificial abrasion [filing] immediately sprang to the eye. Indeed so obvious did they seem it may well be asked—how was it that they had escaped notice before?" The age-stain was better done, but the imported mammalian fossils and hand-crafted tools were again obvious frauds. People *wanted* to believe in evolution, so they were able to see what they *wanted to believe* (a "people problem" that can only be solved by honestly looking at alternate sides of an issue).

Sometimes people ask me how virtually all the evolutionists in the world could be so wrong about such an important issue as human origins. Answer: it wouldn't be the first time. Science is a human endeavor, and human beings make mistakes. Evolution goes far beyond the limits of science, and is even more easily influenced by human bias. I know that both intellectually and personally since I once accepted the evolutionary bias and its view of the evidence.

The "human factor" in the study of human origins is apparent in the multiple and varied interpretations of Java and Peking Man (*"Homo erectus"*) recounted in a very readable, yet thoroughly documented, book by Marvin Lubenow, *Bones of Contention*.[6]

Joining Neanderthals, Blacks, Aborigines, and Piltdown Man as proposed witnesses for human evolution at the famous Scopes trial in 1925 was Nebraska Man. Nebraska Man was dignified by the scientific name *Hesperopithecus haroldcookii*, but he was never known by anything but a tooth. By imagination, the tooth was

A. *Neanderthals* turned out to be just plain people, some of whom suffered from bone diseases. In proper attire, they would attract no particular attention today.

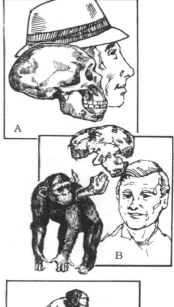

B. *Piltdown Man (Eoanthropus dawsoni)* was a deliberate (but not very clever) hoax palmed off as "proof of evolution" to students for more than two generations. It turned out to be a bit of ape jaw and human skull artificially aged.

C. *Nebraska Man (Hesperopithecus)* was reconstructed, family and all, from a tooth—a tooth that later was found to belong to a pig!

put in a skull, the skull was put on a skeleton, and the skeleton was given flesh, hair, and a family! Figure 1 includes a picture of Nebraska Man redrawn from a London newspaper published during the year of the Scopes trial.

Two years later, Nebraska Man was back to being just a tooth. The tooth was found in the real skull, attached to the real skeleton. It turned out not to be the tooth of man's ape-like ancestor, but the tooth of an extinct pig!

Most evolutionists have long since learned not to make so much of a tooth. Yet it was not until 1979 that *Ramapithecus*—"reconstructed as a biped on the basis of teeth and jaws alone"—was dropped as a "false start of the human parade" (Zihlman and Lowenstein[7]). That didn't stop Elwyn Simons[8] from suggesting that *Aegyptopithecus* is a "nasty little thing" whose social behavior and family life—conjured up largely from eye sockets and the canine teeth of the males—are supposed to make it a kind of psychological ancestor of man!

The Australian National Museum in Sydney has apparently found a solution to the problem of evolutionary links still missing between apes and man. In June of 1993, we were greeted by a display describing five kinds of apes: lemurs, orangs, gorillas, chimps, and man. No need to look for links between apes and mankind if human beings are *still* apes! One display, described nursing behavior in various apes, including people. Another showed that man and chimps are the only apes that murder their own kind. A third pictured love-making among people and other apes. The text mentioned that some apes were monogamous, others polygamous or promiscuous, and that some men were like gorillas, others like chimps, etc. It was a truly inspiring and edifying display! Most evolutionists, of course, would be just as disgusted by the displays as would anyone else with a respect for science (or for common sense).

Modern speculation on mankind's ancestry centers on a group of fossils called *Australopithecus*. In the public mind, these fossils are associated especially with the work in Africa of the Leakey family and of Donald Johanson and his famous specimen, "Lucy" (Figure 2).

The name *Australopithecus* means "southern ape," and it seems that apes are just what they are. Johanson likes to point out that where he finds his australopithecine bones, he finds many of the regular African animals (rhinos, boas, hippos, monkeys, etc.), but never apes. Could it be that apes are exactly what he has been finding all along? Its features are clearly ape-like—except that some claim Lucy and other australopithecines walked upright.

But how crucial to the definition of man is relatively upright posture? Vincent Sarich at the University of California in Berkeley and Adrienne Zihlman say that if you want something that walks upright, consider the living pygmy chimpanzee, *Pan paniscus*. This rare, rain-forest chimpanzee is only slightly shorter than the average chimpanzee, but it spends a fair amount of time walking upright. (I've watched them in the San Diego Zoo.) Since all the other features of the australopithecines are so apelike, perhaps Johanson and the Leakeys have discovered the ancestor of the living pygmy chimpanzee!

But did the australopithecines indeed walk upright? In the *American Biology Teacher,* Charles Oxnard[9] says:

> In one sense you may think there is no problem. For most anthropologists are agreed that the gracile australopithecines ... are on the main human lineage .... This is the view that is presented in almost all textbooks; I expect that it has been your teaching in the classroom; and it is widely broadcast in such publications as the "Time-Life Series" and the beautiful [television] story of "The Ascent of Man." However, anatomical features in some of these fossils provide a warning against a too-ready acceptance of this story . . . .

As part of his warning, Oxnard reminds his readers of gross errors once made in the cases of Piltdown Man and Nebraska Man.

Oxnard then proceeds to examine the evidence. And he's well qualified to do so as Professor of Anatomy at the University of Southern California. He points out first that anatomical relationships cannot be simply established by subjective opinion. Viewed

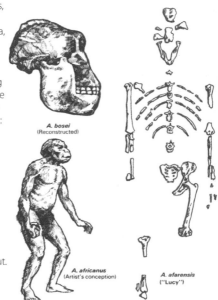

Figure 2. Australopithecines, including Johanson's "Lucy" and the Leakey finds in Africa, are the current candidates for man's ancestors. But USC's Charles Oxnard says the fossils "provide a warning against too ready acceptance of this view." He reaches two conclusions. One is scientific: "If the australopithecines walked upright, it was not in the human manner." The second is educational: "Be critical." We must encourage our science students to examine evidence more critically, he says—and, I might add, that's what the two-model creation-evolution concept is all about.

A. bosei (Reconstructed)

A. africanus (Artist's conception)

A. afarensis ("Lucy")

one way, for example, the pelvic bones of australopithecines seem to be intermediate between man and ape. But merely viewing the bones from a different angle makes the specimen seem as far distant from man as the other apes are. "Yet another view," says Oxnard, "might suggest that the fossil arose from the African apes via modern humans!"—in other words, that *humans* were the missing link between the apes and the australopithecines!

Because he is so sensitive to the serious problems of subjective interpretations, Oxnard then goes on to describe in fascinating detail a computer technique called "multivariate analysis." He goes into both its practical and its theoretic applications and reaches two conclusions.

First, his scientific conclusion: if the australopithecines walked upright, it was *not* in the human manner. If their posture resembled that of any living creature, it was most likely the orangutan. Oxnard also reaches a second conclusion for educators: "*Be critical.*" That is, examine all the relevant evidence. Look at it from different viewpoints. That's really the only way we can protect ourselves against bias in science or any other human endeavor: a willingness to constantly check assumptions and to listen respectfully to the views of others. I trust that's what we're doing in this book, and I wish students around the world had the same freedom to explore both sides of the creation-evolution issue.

Louis Leakey started the modern interest in australopithecines (and captured the attention of *National Geographic*) way back in 1959 with his "ape man," *Zinjanthropus*. *Zinjanthropus* has since been reclassified as *Australopithecus bosei*, and it is now considered grossly apelike, an extinct ape really not related to man at all.

In fact, it was not the skeletal features that attracted attention to the Leakey finds in the first place. It was tools. Tools imply a tool maker. Since the tools were found with *Australopithecus*, Louis Leakey assumed that that creature had made the tools. Thirteen years later, Richard Leakey found beneath the bones his father had unearthed "bones virtually indistinguishable from those of modern man." Perhaps that solved the tool-maker mystery. At the time, Richard Leakey said his discovery shattered standard beliefs in evolution.

Actually, fossil discoveries have been *shattering* standard beliefs in evolution with monotonous regularity. Each in its day was hailed as "scientific proof" that human beings evolved from apelike animals, yet all the candidates once proposed as our evolutionary ancestors have been knocked off the list. The cover story in *Time* magazine for March 14, 1994, *assumes* that evolution is an absolute fact,[10] but it summarizes what is really the evaporating case for human evolution with these dramatic words:

Figure 3. Footprints are more distinctive of man than most bone fragments are. If the footprints above are accepted as human, evolutionists would have to say that man existed "before" man's supposed ancestors. Creationists say that these footprints (and the Castenedolo and Kanapoi bones) simply suggest that people have always been people, beginning with the first created human beings.

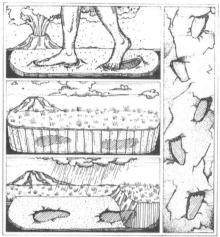

Yet despite more than a century of digging, the fossil record remains *maddeningly sparse*. With so few clues, even *a single bone* that doesn't fit into the picture *can upset everything*. Virtually every major discovery has put *deep cracks* in the conventional wisdom and forced scientists to *concoct new theories*, amid furious debate. [Emphasis added.]

It's sad that human evolution is still taught as "fact" to school children, college students, and the general public, when "virtually every major discovery" has discredited the so-called evidence and disproved the theory. Even sadder, scientists who know the evidence and are "forced to concoct new theories" are only concocting new theories of *how* human evolution occurred, unwilling to ask *whether* evolution occurred and to work on the truly new, non-evolutionary theories that the evidence demands.

The australopithecines could not have been our ancestors, of course, if *people* were walking around *before* Lucy and her kin were fossilized—and there is evidence to suggest just that. Fossils of ordinary people in mid-Tertiary rock were found in Castenidolo,

Italy, back in the late 1800s, and the evolutionist Sir Arthur Keith recognized that accepting these "pre-ape" finds would shatter his belief in evolution (or at least its scientific support). Oxnard[11] and Lubenow[12] call attention to the *Kanapoi hominid*, a human upper arm bone found in rock strata in Africa laid down *before* those that entomb the australopithecine remains.

Then there's the footprint evidence. Actually, we have many features in common with the apes (as a trip to the zoo will verify), and it should not be surprising that some bones would be difficult to classify. But apes and human beings have quite different footprints. The apes have essentially "four hands," with an opposable big toe that makes their footprint quite different from ours. They also have a gait that's quite different and a tendency to drop to all fours and "knuckle walk."

In *National Geographic*[13] and *Science News*,[14] Mary Leakey describes a trail of man-like prints in volcanic ash near Laetoli in east Africa. Figure 3, redrawn from the former, shows Mary Leakey's concept of how the prints were formed and preserved and the kind of foot that made them. If you examine the article, you'll find that the foot looks pretty much like yours or mine.

In the center of the *National Geographic* article is a two-page fold out. Elephants, giraffes, guinea hens, and acacia trees dot the scene. Except for the volcano, it looks as if it could have been taken from a Tarzan movie. Then across the center is a line of very human-like tracks. You might be surprised, however, at what the artist put *in* the tracks. An artist had to do it, by the way, since we have no foot bones connected to leg bones, etc., to tell us what really made the tracks. Perhaps the most logical inference from these observations is that people made them. The stride is quite short, but perhaps the person was small or just very cautious about walking across the damp volcanic ash.

Most evolutionists, however, forbid themselves to believe that these tracks could be made by people, because they don't believe people evolved until later. The Kanapoi hominid, however, suggests that people might very well have been around to make these prints. And living not far from that site in Africa today are people (the Pygmies) not much taller as adults than the Laetoli print-makers.

Understanding the serious implications of the Laetoli finds, one scientist looked almost desperately for evidence that some animal, and not man, may have made those prints. He even had a dancing bear jump up and down in mud, hoping those tracks would resemble the Laetoli prints! His conclusion? It was impossible to tell the Laetoli tracks from ordinary human footprints. As an evolutionist, he used such adjectives as "shocking," "disturbing," and "upsetting" to describe his results, since none of the popular evolutionary "links," including Lucy, could be man's ancestor, if people were already walking around before these so-called ancestors were fossilized. To the creationist, the evidence simply confirms that *people have always been people, and apes always apes, as far back as the evidence goes.*

[This chapter is an excerpt from *Creation: Facts of Life* by Gary Parker, published by Master Books, 2006]

1.   Jerry Adler and John Carey, "Is Man a Subtle Accident?" *Newsweek*, November 3, 1980.

2.   Thomas Kelly (producer), *Puzzle of the Ancient Wing*, Canadian Broadcasting Corporation: "Man Alive" television series, 1981.

3.   Henry Osborn, "The Evolution of Human Races," *Natural History*, April 1980. (Reprinted from *Natural History*, January/February 1926).

4.   Stephen Jay Gould, "The Brain Appraisers," *Science Digest*, September 1981.

5.   Stephen Jay Gould, "Smith Woodward's Folly," *New Scientist*, April 5, 1979.

6.   Marvin Lubenow, *Bones of Contention* (Grand Rapids: Baker Books 1992).

7.   Adrienne Zihlman and Jerold Lowenstein, "False Start of the Human Parade," *Natural History*, August/September 1979.

8.   Elwyn Simons, "Just a Nasty Little Thing," as quoted in *Time*, February 18, 1980.

9.   Charles E. Oxnard, "Human Fossils: New View of Old Bones," *American Biology Teacher*, May 1979.

10.   Michael Lemonick, "How Man Began." *Time*, March 14, 1994.

11.   Oxnard, "Human Fossils: New View of Old Bones," 1979.

12. Lubenow, *Bones of Contention*, 1992.

13. Mary D. Leakey, "Footprints in the Ashes of Time," *National Geographic*, April 1979.

14. Mary D. Leakey, "Happy Trail for Three Hominids," *Science News*, February 9, 1980.

Gary Parker began his teaching career as an atheist and evolutionist. En route to his degrees in biology/chemistry, biology/physiology, and then an EdD in biology/geology (Ball State), Dr Parker earned several academic awards, including admission to Phi Beta Kappa (the prestigious national scholastic society), election to the American Society of Zoologists (for his research on tadpoles), and a fifteen-month fellowship award from the National Science Foundation. He has published five programmed textbooks in biology and six books on origins science (the latter have been translated into eight languages), has appeared in numerous films/television programs, and has debated and lectured worldwide on creation.

What About the Similarity Between Human and Chimp DNA?

by David A. DeWitt

The first thing I want to do is clear up a common misconception—especially among many within the Church. Many falsely believe that in an evolutionary worldview humans evolved from chimpanzees. And so they ask, "If humans came from chimps, then why are there still chimps?" However, this is not a good question to ask because an evolutionary worldview does not teach this. The evolutionists commonly teach that humans and chimpanzees are both basically "cousins" and have a common ancestor in our past. If you go back far enough *all* life likely has a single common ancestor in the evolutionary view. This, of course, does not mesh with Genesis 1–2.

Evolutionists frequently assert that the similarity in DNA sequences provides evidence that all organisms (especially humans and chimps) are descended from a common ancestor. However, DNA similarity could just as easily be explained as the result of a common Creator.

Human designers frequently reuse the same elements and features, albeit with modifications. Since all living things share the same world, it should be expected that there would be similarities in DNA as the organisms would have similar needs. Indeed, it would be quite surprising if every living thing had completely different sequences for each protein—especially ones which carried out the same function.

Organisms that have highly similar functionality and physiological needs would be expected to have a degree of DNA similarity.

What is DNA?

Every living cell contains DNA (deoxyribonucleic acid) which provides the hereditary instructions for living things to survive, grow, and reproduce. The DNA is comprised of chemicals called bases, which are paired and put together in double-stranded chains. There are four different bases which are represented by the letters A, T, C, and G. Because A is always paired with T and C is always paired with G, one strand of DNA can serve as a template for producing the other strand.

The DNA is transcribed into a single chain of nucleotides called RNA (ribonucleic acid) which is then translated into the amino acid sequence of a protein. In this way, the sequence of bases in DNA determines the sequence of amino acids in a protein which in turn determines the protein structure and function.

In the human genome (total genetic information in the nucleus of the cell), there are roughly 3 billion base pairs of DNA with

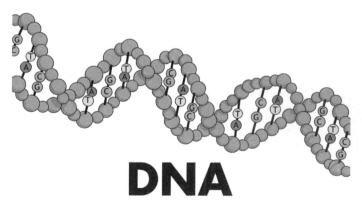

The double-stranded DNA molecule forms with an A opposite a T and a G opposite a C. This sequence determines the structure of proteins.

about 20,000 genes (regions that code for proteins). Surprisingly, only about 1% of the DNA actually codes for proteins. The rest is non-coding DNA. Some of this DNA comprises control areas—segments of DNA responsible for turning genes on and off, controlling the amount and timing of protein production. There are also portions of DNA that play structural roles. Still other regions of DNA have as-yet unknown functions.

What is the real percent similarity between humans and chimpanzees?

Ever since the time of Darwin, evolutionary scientists have noted the anatomical (physical/visible) similarities between humans and the great apes including chimpanzees, gorillas, and orangutans. Over the last few decades, molecular biologists have joined the fray, pointing out the similarities in DNA sequences. Previous estimates of genetic similarity between humans and chimpanzees suggested they were 98.5–99.4% identical.[1]

Because of this similarity, evolutionists have viewed the chimpanzee as "our closest living relative." Most early comparative studies were carried out only on genes (such as the sequence of the cytochrome c protein), which constituted only a very tiny fraction of the roughly 3 billion DNA base pairs that comprise our genetic blueprint. Although the full human genome sequence has been available since 2001, the whole chimpanzee genome has not. Thus, much of the previous work was based on only a fraction of the total DNA.

In the fall of 2005, in a special issue of *Nature* devoted to chimpanzees, researchers reported the draft sequence of the chimpanzee genome.[2] At the time, some researchers called it "the most dramatic confirmation yet"[3] of Darwin's theory that man shared a common ancestor with the apes. One headline read: "Charles Darwin was right and chimp gene map proves it."[4]

So what is this great and overwhelming "proof" of chimp-human common ancestry? Researchers found 96% genetic similarity and a difference between us of 4%. This is a very strange kind of proof because it is actually double the percent difference that evolutionists have claimed for years![5] Even so, no matter what the actual percent difference turned out to be, whether 2%, 4%, or 10%, they still would have claimed that Darwin was right to support their worldview.

Further, the use of percentages obscures the magnitude of the differences. For example, 1.23% of the differences are single base pair substitutions.[6] This doesn't sound like much until you realize that it represents about 35 million differences! But that is only the beginning. There are 40–45 million bases present in humans that are missing from chimps and about the same number present in chimps that are absent from man. These extra DNA nucleotides are called "insertions" or "deletions" because they are thought to have been added to or lost from the original sequence. (Substitutions and insertions are compared at right.) This puts the total number of DNA differences at about 125 million. However, since the insertions can be more than one nucleotide long, there are about 40 million total separate mutation events that would separate the two species in the evolutionary view.

To put this number into perspective, a typical 8½ x 11 page of text might have 4,000 letters and spaces. It would take 10,000 such pages full of text to equal 40 million letters! So the difference between humans and chimpanzees includes about 35 million DNA bases that are different, about 45 million in the human that are absent from the chimp, and about 45 million in the chimp that are absent from the human.

Creationists believe that God made Adam directly from the dust of the earth just as the Bible says in Genesis 2. Therefore, man and the apes have never had an ancestor in common. Assuming they did, for the sake of analyzing the argument, then 40 million separate

A	A		A	A
G	G		G	G
T	T		T	T
C	C		C	C
G	A		A	
T	T		T	T
A	A		A	A
C	C		C	C
C	C		C	C

| Substitution | Insertion/deletion |

Comparison between a base substitution and an insertion/deletion. Two DNA sequences can be compared. If there is a difference in the nucleotides (e.g., an A instead of a G) at a given position this is a substitution. In contrast, if there is a nucleotide base which is missing it is considered an insertion/deletion. It is assumed that a nucleotide has been inserted into one of the sequences or one has been deleted from the other. It is often too difficult to determine whether the difference is a result of an insertion or a deletion and thus it is called an "indel." Indels can be of virtually any length.

mutation events would have had to take place and become fixed in the population in only 300,000 generations. This is an average of 133 mutations locked into the genome every generation. Locking in such a staggering number of mutations in a relatively small number of generations is a problem referred to as "Haldane's dilemma."[7]

The differences make the difference

There are many other differences between chimpanzee and human genomes that are not quantifiable as percentages.[8] Specific examples of these differences include:

At the end of each chromosome is a string of repeating DNA sequences called telomeres. Chimpanzees and other apes have about 23,000 base pairs of DNA at their telomeres. Humans are unique among primates with much shorter telomeres only 10,000 long.[9]

While 18 pairs of chromosomes are virtually identical, chromosomes 4, 9, and 12 show evidence of being "remodeled."[10] In other words, the genes and markers on these chromosomes are not in the same order in the human and chimpanzee. Instead of being "remodeled," as the evolutionists suggest, these could also be intrinsic differences as each was a separate creation.

Even with genetic similarity, there can be differences in the amount of specific proteins produced. Just because DNA sequences are similar does not mean that the same amounts of the proteins are produced. Such differences in protein expression can yield vastly different responses in cells. Roughly 10% of genes examined showed significant differences in expression levels between chimpanzees and humans.[11]

Gene families are groups of genes that have similar sequences and also similar functions. Scientists comparing the number of genes in gene families have revealed significant differences between humans and chimpanzees. Humans have 689 genes that chimps lack and chimps have 86 genes that humans lack. Such differences mean that 6% of the gene complement is different between humans and chimpanzees, irrespective of the individual DNA base pairs.[12]

Thus, the percentage of matching DNA is only one measure of how similar two organisms are, and not really a good one at that. There are other factors besides DNA sequence that determine an organism's phenotype (how traits are physically expressed). Indeed, even though identical twins have the same DNA sequence, as they grow older, twins show differences in protein expression.[13] Therefore, there must be some interaction between the genes and the environment.

Importantly, not all of the data support chimp-human common ancestry as nicely as evolutionists typically suggest. In particular, when scientists made a careful comparison between human, chimpanzee, and gorilla genomes, they found a significant number of genetic markers where humans matched gorillas more closely than chimpanzees! Indeed, at 18–29% of the genetic markers, either humans and gorillas or chimpanzees and gorillas had a closer match to each other than chimpanzees and humans.[14]

These results are certainly not what one would expect according to standard evolutionary theory. Chimpanzees and humans are supposed to share a more recent common ancestor with each other than either have with the gorilla. Trying to account for the unexpected distribution of common markers that would otherwise conflict with evolutionary predictions, the authors of this study made the bizarre suggestion: perhaps chimpanzees and humans split off from a common ancestor, but later descendants of each reproduced to form chimp-human hybrids. Such an "explanation" appears to be an attempt to rescue the concept of chimp-human common ancestry rather than to provide the data to confirm this hypothesis.

All similarities are not equal

A high degree of sequence similarity does not equate to proteins having exactly the same function or role. For example, the FOX2P protein, which has been shown to be involved in language, has only 2 out of about 700 amino acids which are different between chimpanzees and humans.[15] This means they are 99.7% identical. While this might seem like a trivial difference, consider exactly what those differences are. In the FOX2P protein, humans have the amino acid asparagine instead of threonine at position 303 and then a serine that is in place of an asparagine at 325. Although apparently a minor alteration, the second change can make a significant difference in the way the protein functions

---

and is regulated.[16] Thus, a very high degree of sequence similarity can be irrelevant if the amino acid that is different plays a crucial role. Indeed, many genetic defects are the result of a single change in an amino acid. For example, sickle cell anemia results from a valine replacing glutamic acid in the hemoglobin protein. It does not matter that every other amino acid is exactly the same.

Usually people think that differences in amino acid sequence only alter the three dimensional shape of a protein. FOX2P demonstrates how a difference in one amino acid can yield a protein that is regulated differently or has altered functions. Therefore, we should not be too quick to trivialize even very small differences in gene sequences. Further, slight differences in regions that don't code for proteins can impact how protein levels are regulated. This alteration can change the amount of protein that is produced or when it is produced. In such cases, the high degree of similarity is meaningless because of the significant functional differences that result from altered protein levels.

What about similar "junk DNA" in human and chimp DNA?

Evolutionists have suggested that there are "plagiarized mistakes" between the human and chimpanzee genome and that these are best explained by a common ancestor. A teacher who found identical errors on two students' papers would be rightly inclined to believe that the students cheated. The best explanation for two papers with an identical error is that they are both from the same original source. In the same way, some evolutionists have suggested that differences or deactivated genes shared by humans and chimps are best explained by common ancestry. They claim that the only alternative is a Creator who put the same error in two different organisms—a claim they would call incredible.

Evolutionists may consider something to be an error when there is a perfectly good reason that is yet unexplained. They conclude that the error is the result of an ancient mutation based on evolutionary assumptions. Further, when it comes to DNA, there may be genetic hotspots that are prone to the same mutation. For example, humans and guinea pigs share alleged mistakes in the vitamin C pseudogene without sharing a recent common ancestor.[17]

Examples of the alleged "plagiarized mistakes" are endogenous retroviruses (ERVs)—part of the so-called "junk DNA." ERVs are stretches of DNA that can be spliced (cut out), copied, and inserted into other locations within the genome. There are many different types of these mobile pieces of DNA.[18]

The ERVs are not always consistent with evolutionary expectations. For example, scientists analyzed the complement component C4 genes (an aspect of the immune system) in a variety of primates.[19] Both chimpanzees and gorillas had short C4 genes. The human gene was long because of an ERV. Interestingly, orangutans and green monkeys had the same ERV inserted at exactly the same point. This is especially significant because humans are supposed to have a more recent common ancestor with both chimpanzees and gorillas and only more distantly with orangutans. Yet the same ERV in exactly the same position would imply that humans and orangutans had the more recent common ancestor. Here is a good case where ERVs do not line up with the expected evolutionary progression. Nonetheless, they are still held up as evidence for common ancestry.

Additional evidence has suggested that ERVs may in fact have functions.[20] One very important function has to do with implantation during pregnancy.[21]

What about the alleged fusion of human chromosome 2?

Humans normally have 23 pairs of chromosomes while chimpanzees have 24. Evolutionary scientists believe that human chromosome 2 has been formed through the fusion of two small chromosomes in an ape-like ancestor in the human lineage instead of an intrinsic difference resulting from a separate creation. While this may account for the difference in chromosome number, a clear and practical mechanism for how a chromosomal abnormality becomes universal in such a large population is lacking. The fusion would have occurred once in a single individual. Every single human being on earth would have to be a descendant of that one individual. Because there is no selective advantage to a fused chromosome, this becomes even more difficult for evolutionists to explain since natural selection would not be a factor.

Evolution proponents who insist that the chromosome 2 fusion event proves that humans and chimpanzees shared a common ancestor are employing a logical fallacy known as affirming the consequent. Affirming the consequent follows the pattern:

If P, then Q

Q

Therefore, P

In other words,

If humans and chimpanzees share a common ancestor, then there will be evidence of chromosome fusion.

There is evidence of chromosome fusion.

Therefore, humans and chimpanzees share a common ancestor.

Here is why it is a logical fallacy: For the sake of the argument, let us assume that humans are descended from ancestors that had 48 chromosomes just like the apes, and that there was a common ancestor 5 million years ago. The alleged chromosome 2 fusion would have occurred after the human line split from that of chimpanzees and been passed to all humans on the planet. Even in an evolutionary scenario, the chromosome fusion does not provide evidence for continuity between humans and chimps because it only links those individuals that share the fusion.[22]

In other words, there is no extra evidence for humans having an ancestor in common with chimpanzees provided by the fusion of chromosome 2. It is no more compelling than it would be if humans and chimpanzees had the same number—48. One could even argue that common ancestry with chimpanzees is *less* compelling because of the alleged fusion on chromosome 2.

Conclusion

The similarity between human and chimpanzee DNA is really in the eye of the beholder. If you look for similarities, you can find them. But if you look for differences, you can find those as well. There are significant differences between the human and chimpanzee genomes that are not easily accounted for in an evolutionary scenario.

Creationists expect both similarities and differences, and that is exactly what we find. The fact that many humans, chimps, and other creatures share genes should be no surprise to the Christian. The differences are significant. Many in the evolutionary world like to discuss the similarities while brushing the differences aside. Emphasis on percent DNA similarity misses the point because it ignores both the magnitude of the actual differences as well as the significance of the role that single amino acid changes can play.

Please consider the implications of the worldviews that are in conflict regarding the origin of mankind. The Bible teaches that man was uniquely formed and made in the image of God (Genesis 1 and 2). The Lord directly fashioned the first man Adam from dust and the first woman Eve from Adam's side. He was intimately involved from the beginning and is still intimately involved. Keep in mind that the Lord Jesus Christ stepped into history to become a man—not a chimp—and now offers the free gift of salvation to those who receive Him.

1. For example: D. E. Wildman et al., "Implications of Natural Selection in Shaping 99.4% Nonsynonymous DNA Identity between Humans and Chimpanzees: Enlarging Genus *Homo*," *Proc. Natl. Acad. Sci.* 100 no. 12 (2003): 7181–7188.

2. The Chimpanzee Sequencing and Analysis Consortium 2005, "Initial Sequence of the Chimpanzee Genome and Comparison with the Human Genome," *Nature* 437 (2005): 69–87.

3. Alan Boyle, "Chimp Genetic Code Opens Human Frontiers," MSNBC, http://www.msnbc.msn.com/id/9136200.

4. The Medical News, "Charles Darwin Was Right and Chimp Gene Map Proves It," http://www.news-medical.net/news/2005/08/31/12840.aspx.

5. Studies of chimp-human similarity have typically ignored insertions and deletions although these account for most of the differences. A study by Roy Britten included these insertions and deletions and obtained a figure that is close to the 4% reported for the full sequence. See Roy J. Britten, "Divergence between Samples of Chimpanzee and Human DNA Sequence Is 5% Counting Indels," *Proc. Nat. Acad. Sci.* 99 no. 21 (2002): 13633–13635.

6. Individuals within a population are variable and some chimps will have more or fewer nucleotide differences with humans. This variation accounts for a portion of the differences. 1.06% are believed to be fixed differences. Fixed differences represent those that are universal. In other words, all chimpanzees have a given nucleotide and all humans have a different one at the same position.

7. Walter J. ReMine, "Cost Theory and the Cost of Substitution—A Clarification," *TJ* 19 no. 1 (2005): 113–125. Note also: This problem is exacerbated because most of the differences between the two organisms are likely due to neutral or random genetic drift. That refers to change in which natural selection is not operating. Without a selective advantage, it is difficult to explain how this huge number of mutations could become fixed in both populations. Instead, many of these may actually be intrinsic sequence differences present from the beginning of creation.

8. Discussed in D. A. DeWitt, "Greater than 98% Chimp/Human DNA Similarity? Not Any More," *TJ* 17 no. 1 (2003): 8–10.

9. S. Kakuo, K. Asaoka, and T. Ide, "Human Is a Unique Species among Primates in Terms of Telomere Length," *Biochem. Biophys. Res. Commun.* 263 (1999): 308–314.

10. Ann Gibbons, "Which of Our Genes Make Us Human?" *Science* 281 (1998): 1432–1434.

11. Y. Gilad et al., "Expression Profiling in Primates Reveals a Rapid Evolution of Human Transcription Factors," *Nature* 440 (2006): 242–245.

12. J. P. Demuth et al., "The Evolution of Mammalian Gene Families," PLoS ONE 1 no. 1 (2006): e85, http://www.plosone.org/article/info:doi%2F10.1371%2Fjournal.pone.0000085.

13. M. F. Fraga et al., "Epigenetic Differences Arise during the Lifetime of Monozygotic Twins," *Proc. Natl. Acad. Sci.* 102 no. 30 (2005): 10,604–10,609.

14. N. Patterson et al., "Genetic Evidence for Complex Speciation of Humans and Chimpanzees," *Nature* 441 (2006): 315–321.

15. W. Enard et al., "Molecular Evolution of FOXP2, a Gene Involved in Speech and Language," *Nature* 418 (2002): 869–872.

16. This difference in amino acid sequence opens up a potential phosphorylation site for protein kinase C. Phosphorylation is a major mechanism for regulating the activity of enzymes as well as transcription factors.

17. Y. Inai, Y. Ohta, and M. Nishikimi, "The Whole Structure of the Human Nonfunctional L-Gulono-Gamma-Lactone Oxidase Gene—the Gene Responsible for Scurvy—and the Evolution of Repetitive Sequences Theron," *J Nutr Sci Vitimol* 49 (2003): 315–319.

18. Humans have many more short interspersed elements (SINEs) than chimps, but chimps have two novel families of retroviral elements, which are absent from man. Comparing endogenous "retroviral elements" yielded 73 human-specific insertions and 45 chimpanzee-specific insertions. Humans have two SINE (Alu) families that the chimpanzees lack and humans have significantly more copies (approx.7,000 human-specific copies vs. approx. 2,300 chimpanzee-specific ones). There are also approx. 2,000 lineage specific L1 elements. All of these lineage specific changes would be required to take place sometime between the last chimp/human common ancestor and the most recent common ancestor for all people on the planet. Importantly, these are modifications for which there is no known selective advantage.

19. A. W. Dangel et al., "Complement Component C4 Gene Intron 9 Has a Phylogenetic Marker for Primates: Long Terminal Repeats of the Endogenous Retrovirus ERV-K(C4) Are a Molecular Clock of Evolution," *Immunogenetics* 42 no. 1 (1995): 41–52.

20. Georgia Purdom, "Human Endogenous Retroviruses (HERVs) – Evolutionary "Junk" or God's Tools?" http://www.answersingenesis.org/docs2006/1219herv.asp.

21. K. A. Dunlap et al., "Endogenous Retroviruses Regulate Periimplantation Placental Growth and Differentiation," *Proc. Nat. Acad. Sci.* 103 no. 29 (2006): 14,390–14,395.

22. There is debate among creationists as to whether the evidence for a chromosome 2 fusion event in humans is compelling. Some believe it is an intrinsic difference; others are open to it occurring early in human history, perhaps shortly before Noah. In both cases, evidence linking humans to chimpanzees based on chromosome fusion is lacking.

David A. DeWitt received a BS in biochemistry from Michigan State University and a PhD in neuroscience from Case Western Reserve University. Currently a professor of biology at Liberty University, he is active in teaching and research. Liberty University recognized Dr DeWitt with the 2000-2001 President's Award for Teaching Excellence.

His primary research efforts have been to understand the mechanisms causing cellular damage in Alzheimer's disease. He has authored and co-authored articles that have appeared in peer-reviewed journals such as *Brain Research* and *Experimental Neurology*.

Dr. DeWitt also serves as the director of the Center for Creation Studies at Liberty University. He has written articles and given many presentations on creation/evolution issues. His interest in creation has focused on molecular and cell biology as well as human origins. He is a member of the Society for Neuroscience, the Creation Research Society, and served as chair of the biology section of the Virginia Academy of Sciences.

Skeleton of a Neanderthal taken before entering La grotte de Clamcuse in France.
© istockphoto.com | fanelie rosier

The Neanderthal: Our Worthy Ancestors

by Marvin Lubenow

One hundred and fifty years have passed since the first Neanderthal fossil individual was discovered in 1856 in the Neander Valley in Germany. Fossil remains of more than 490 Neanderthal individuals have now been recovered. We should know them quite well. Not only do we have more fossils of them and more of their artifacts than of any other fossil group, but they also lived, allegedly, in the most recent times before modern humans. Yet to evolutionists, they are still mysterious, with many questions about them still unanswered.

To young-earth creationists, the Neanderthals are not mysterious, but rather incredibly intriguing. We view the Neanderthals as the fully human ancestors of some modern humans, probably some Europeans and western Asians, where the Neanderthals lived. Hence, we creationists would refer to them as *Homo sapiens sapiens*, or as a sub-species of modern humans: *Homo sapiens neanderthalensis*. Either way, we believe that they would be fully capable of reproducing with modern humans if they were living today. They were a post-Flood, Ice Age people, specializing in hunting the large, grazing animals that were abundant towards the end of the Ice Age and afterwards.

When the Neanderthals were first discovered, they were considered to be a separate species, *Homo neanderthalensis*. Since reproductive capability is on the species level, the significance of the original designation was that they were considered different enough from modern humans so as to not be able to reproduce with us.

In the 1960s, new studies on the Neanderthals properly revealed that their skeletal distinctions were not that significant and they were given sub-species status with modern humans, *Homo sapiens neanderthalensis*. That situation persisted until it became possible to study DNA in fossil bones. Based on this fossil DNA research, paleoanthropologists now claim that the Neanderthals were a species separate and distinct from modern humans. In this chapter, we will examine first the DNA evidence, then the fossil evidence, and finally the archaeological evidence to see that Neanderthals were fully human.

The DNA evidence

A turning point in DNA research was the discovery of techniques to identify and manipulate genetic material by using the polymerase chain reaction (PCR). This discovery was such a remarkable breakthrough in modern biotechnology that Kary B. Mullis shared the 1993 Nobel prize for chemistry for inventing the technique.

Before PCR, there was a shortage of genetic material for experiments. This material was extremely difficult to obtain because it was always embedded in a living cell. It was hard to get an intact molecule of natural DNA from any organism except from extremely simple viruses. The PCR technique enables researchers to make unlimited copies of any specific DNA sequence independent of the organism from which it came.

Because DNA, the genetic code, is such an incredibly complex molecule, when an organism dies its DNA breaks down rather rapidly. Eventually the strands of the molecule are so short that no information can be obtained from them. PCR, with its ability to replicate short strands of DNA, opened the door to the possibility of obtaining genetic information from fossil material, even though that material was degraded. Hence the successful recovery of mitochondrial DNA (mtDNA) from the Neanderthal skeleton from the Neander Valley, Germany. This dramatic recovery was announced in the journal *Cell* on July 11, 1997.

Because that recovery revealed differences between Neanderthal mtDNA and modern human mtDNA, evolutionists interpreted the results to mean that the Neanderthal line separated from the line leading to modern humans about 600,000 years ago and that the Neanderthals died out without passing on any mtDNA to modern humans. The implications are that the Neanderthals did not evolve into modern humans and that they were a totally different species from modern humans.

In spite of the brilliance of recovering mtDNA from a Neanderthal fossil, there are flaws in the basic assumption, in the methodology, and in the interpretation of the results of the recovery. We will cover just some of these matters briefly.

1. *The mtDNA recovery is flawed in its basic assumptions.* In dealing with this Neanderthal specimen, the scientific team searched for mtDNA rather than for nuclear DNA. There are only two copies of DNA in the nucleus of each cell, but there is an average of 750 copies of mtDNA in each cell. Thus, the possibility was greater that some of the Neanderthal mtDNA might be preserved. Unlike nuclear DNA, *evolutionists have assumed that mtDNA passes without change from a mother to her offspring.* Since all changes in mtDNA are believed to result from mutations rather than from genetic recombination with the father, evolutionists believe that mtDNA is a more accurate record of evolutionary history. Furthermore, since mtDNA is unable to repair itself, mtDNA mutations occur at about ten times the rate of nuclear DNA, making it, they believe, a more precise record of time.

The *crucial* assumption in the practice of building evolutionary family trees on the basis of mtDNA is *the belief that mtDNA is passed on only through the mother* and hence all changes in the mtDNA are mutations upon which one can build a timeline of evolutionary history. This assumption has been shown by experimentation to be *false* by one of the world's leading evolutionary biologists, the late John Maynard Smith (Sussex University). It is reinforced by experiments by other biologists. Smith has expressed frustration that the evolutionary establishment has ignored these findings.[1] The reason for this attitude toward the new evidence is that a huge body of literature has arisen dealing with evolutionary relationships based upon mtDNA. Since evolutionists believe that this gives them the "proof" for evolution that they have sought for 150 years, giving up this belief is like asking an addict to give up his habit. The older tests were not sensitive enough to reveal that some of the father's mtDNA is also passed on. The newer tests, thanks to PCR, reveal that the father's mtDNA is also passed on to the offspring, therefore *invalidating all evolutionary trees and timetables based upon mtDNA*. Evolutionists have ignored the newer data.

2. *The mtDNA recovery is flawed in the interpretation of the data.* Based upon a difference of about 0.123%[2] between the Neanderthal and modern human mtDNA, the experimenters claim that the Neanderthals and modern humans are two distinct species. That claim implies that we know how many mtDNA substitutions it would take to separate one species from another. Maryellen Ruvolo (Harvard University) points out that the genetic variation between the modern and Neanderthal sequences is within the range of other single species of primates. She goes on to say: ". . . there isn't a yardstick for genetic difference upon which you can define a species."[3] In other words, we do not know how many mtDNA substitutions it would take between Neanderthals and modern humans to make fertility impossible. *Species distinctions are based on mating compatibility, not on the number of mtDNA differences.* Hence, the claim that the Neanderthals are a separate species has no factual basis and could only have been a subjective decision.

3. *The mtDNA recovery is flawed in its methodology.* Flaw #1: The ability to study genetic material with the help of PCR is an

amazing success story. However, there is one serious problem. In analyzing ancient DNA (or mtDNA) there is always the serious problem of contamination from modern DNA. This contamination could come from the hundreds who have handled this particular Neanderthal fossil since its discovery in 1856, from laboratory personnel, from laboratory equipment, and even from the heating and cooling system in the laboratory. Even a single cell of modern human contamination would have its DNA amplified blindly and preferentially by the PCR because of its superior state of preservation over the older Neanderthal DNA. As DNA authority Tomas Lindahl puts it: the PCR technique is "notoriously contamination-sensitive."[4] During the recovery, transportation, and study of any fossil, many humans would normally handle it. Yet, even when every precaution is taken to cleanse a fossil of contaminating modern human DNA, the problem is so serious that some contamination from modern DNA is impossible to avoid.

If, for instance, one is using PCR to recover dinosaur DNA in a dinosaur fossil, some contaminating human DNA will show up. Since one does not expect to find human DNA in a dinosaur, it is very logical to assume that all human DNA that is found in the dinosaur DNA recovery is from human contamination.

However, the closer the target DNA is (in this case Neanderthal mtDNA) to modern human mtDNA, the more difficult the problem of discrimination becomes. In other words, it is much easier to recognize modern human DNA contamination in ancient *non-human* specimens than in ancient *human* specimens. The *closer* ancient human DNA sequences are to modern ones, the harder it is to tell if they are truly ancient or if they are the result of modern human contamination. The fossil evidence shows that the Neanderthals were closely related to anatomically modern humans. Hence, it would be normal to expect that their DNA would be quite similar also. It is in this area of seeking to discriminate between (1) genuine ancient Neanderthal DNA and (2) modern human DNA contamination that serious problems can arise. *I saw a serious problem* as I studied the methodology used by the authors of the *Cell* article.

The *Cell* article reveals some rather strange assumptions. In the PCR amplifications, the researchers obtained both (1) modern human mtDNA, which they assumed, without proof, to be *entirely* contamination from modern humans, and (2) mtDNA that was a bit different from modern human mtDNA, which they assumed, without proof, to be the only true ancient Neanderthal mtDNA. They then used specific primers that would amplify only what they believed to be the true ancient Neanderthal mtDNA and that would *not amplify*, that is, *suppress*, the mtDNA that they believed to be modern human contamination. Since it is absolutely impossible to know for sure whether the mtDNA they suppressed was truly contamination or actually a legitimate part of the ancient Neanderthal mtDNA, their skewed methodology *guaranteed* that their results would show that the Neanderthals were some genetic distance from modern humans. And without knowing how much genetic distance was necessary to establish the Neanderthals as a separate species, the *Cell* researchers arbitrarily declared the Neanderthals to be just that—a separate species.

Since I follow these matters very closely, I have been amazed that no one has commented upon what seems to be an obvious flaw in the methodology (except for a tiny item in *Scientific American*). Noting that the results of the mtDNA recovery favor the "Out of Africa" theory, they explain, as I have, how the deck has been stacked:

> But some anthropologists complain that to ensure that the sequences truly come from Neanderthals and not modern contaminants, molecular biologists typically accept as valid only those sequences that lie outside of the modern human range. This requirement thereby stacks the deck against Neanderthals that might have DNA like ours,

which is what those advocating the multiregional evolution theory expect to see.[5]

4. *The mtDNA recovery is flawed in its methodology.* Flaw #2: Repeatability is central to science. It is basic to scientific methodology that any valid experiment must be repeatable under independent conditions. The researchers in the *Cell* article claim that their work had been successfully repeated and verified in a laboratory at The Pennsylvania State University. However, a group of Australian scientists claim that such was not the case. They state that ". . . independent sequence results were not achieved . . . until primers, based on the Neanderthal sequence from the first laboratory, were used . . . ." They emphasize that this does not constitute an independent replication.[6]

5. *Other mtDNA recoveries do not support the* Cell *journal conclusions.* Since the initial mtDNA recovery from the 1856 Neanderthal specimen, there have been a number of other recoveries from fossil humans that seem to indicate that human mtDNA has nothing to do with species distinctions. This includes:

- Two anatomically modern fossil individuals, Cro-Magnon types, from Italy, had mtDNA *very similar* to modern humans living today.[7]

- One anatomically modern fossil individual from Australia, Mungo Man 3, had mtDNA *very different* from modern humans living today.[8]

- Three Neanderthal (*robust morphology*) recoveries showing mtDNA *somewhat different* from modern humans living today.[9]

- Ten Australian fossil individuals having *robust morphology* had mtDNA *very similar* to modern humans living today.[10]

If we assume that these were genuine mtDNA recoveries, the only legitimate conclusion one can make is that mtDNA is not an indicator of human morphology (shape), nor is it an indicator of species distinctions.

6. Species distinctions are normally formed to help define statements about reproductive continuity or discontinuity. Thus we would expect that different species designations would reflect different interpretations of gene flow (reproductivity) between Neanderthals and modern humans. However, a study of various paleoanthropologists' work reveals a lack of consistency in this area. Species definitions are generally ambiguous. While there is spirited debate as to which species designation should be given to the Neanderthals, there is very little debate or information concerning what these species designations actually mean.

For instance, C. Loring Brace (University of Michigan) believes that gene flow took place between the Neanderthals and modern humans, and Ian Tattersall (American Museum of Natural History, New York) believes that no gene flow took place. Thus it seems natural that Brace believes that they represent the same species while Tattersall believes that they represent different species.

However, G. Brauer and Fred H. Smith (Loyola University, Chicago) have similar views regarding gene flow between Neanderthals and modern humans. Yet, they favor different species designations.

Even more confusing is that Christopher Stringer (Natural History Museum, London) is a prime advocate of the "Out of Africa" model of human evolution, while Milford Wolpoff (University of Michigan) is the leading advocate of the Multiregional Continuity model. Consistency would dictate that Stringer should believe in no genetic mixing between the Neanderthals and modern humans, while Wolpoff should believe in a lot of mixing. However, they both agree that some genetic mixing took place between the Neanderthals and modern humans. Yet Stringer believes that they are separate species whereas Wolpoff believes that they belong to the same species.

The fact that most paleoanthropologists believe that the Neanderthals were a separate species and that most of them also believe that the Neanderthals were able to share genes with modern humans represents a basic inconsistency in the interpretation of the human fossil and genetic evidence. The biblical teaching that humans were created in the image of God and reproduce "after their kind" fits well with the fossil record and with the idea that Neanderthals and modern humans are members of the same biblical "kind."[11]

Today, the majority of paleoanthropologists believe that the Neanderthals were a species separate from modern humans. The implication of their being a separate species is that if the Neanderthals were living today, they probably would not be able to reproduce with us. But as we pointed out earlier, most paleoanthropologists also believe that there was at least some degree of cross-fertilization between Neanderthals and modern humans. These two beliefs seem to represent a contradiction in the species concept in human evolution that requires clarification.

DNA studies are the major basis on which the Neanderthals are considered to be a separate species. We also showed in Part I that DNA comparisons do not constitute a proper "tool" by which to determine species relationships. The only "tool" by which to determine species relationships is fertility. Obviously, with fossil individuals, this determination is impossible.

However, there are two lines of evidence, more objective than DNA interpretation, that support the fact that the Neanderthals were fully human ancestors of modern humans, especially Europeans. These lines of evidence are:

1. fossil evidence that Neanderthals lived in close association and integration with modern humans

2. cultural evidence that Neanderthal behavior and thought was fully human.

   The amount of evidence in these two areas is extensive.

The fossil evidence

Neanderthals and modern humans as an integrated population

The "classic" Neanderthal differs somewhat from the typical modern human—the Neanderthal skull is a bit flatter and elongated, the chin is rounder, and the skeleton is more robust. However, there is much overlap. In fact, there should never have been a question about Neanderthal's status in the human family. When the first Neanderthal was discovered in 1856, even "Darwin's bulldog," Thomas Huxley, recognized that it was fully human and not an evolutionary ancestor. Donald Johanson, who discovered the famous fossil, Lucy, writes:

> From a collection of modern human skulls Huxley was able to select a series with features leading "by insensible gradations" from an average modern specimen to the Neanderthal skull. In other words, it wasn't qualitatively different from present-day *Homo sapiens*.[12]

What Huxley discovered 150 years ago—gradations from Neanderthals to modern humans—is clearly seen in the fossil record today. We are not referring to an evolutionary transition from earlier Neanderthals to later modern humans. We are referring to morphological gradations between Neanderthals and modern humans both living at the same time as contemporaries and representing a single human population. Whereas evolutionists have chosen to divide these Europeans into two categories—Neanderthals and anatomically modern *Homo sapiens*, the individual fossils do not fit well into those categories. There is a wide range of variation among modern humans, and there is also much variation within the Neanderthal category. A number of fossils in each group are very close to a subjective line which divides the two groups. The placement of that line is dependent upon the individual paleoanthropologist making the assessment. Since these fossil individuals could be categorized either way, they constitute a seamless gradation between Neanderthals and modern humans. Thus, they demonstrate that the distinction made by evolutionists is an artificial one.

Among fossils usually classified as Neanderthal are at least 26 individuals from six different sites who are clearly close to that subjective line which divides Neanderthals from anatomically modern Homo sapiens. These fossils constitute part of that continuum or gradation. Evolutionists recognize these fossils as departing from the classic Neanderthal morphology and describe them as "progressive" or "advanced" Neanderthals. Their shape is sometimes explained as the result of gene flow (hybridization) with more modern populations. This would conflict with the interpretation of mtDNA and nuclear DNA that the Neanderthals and modern humans are not the same species—since reproduction is on the species level.

Completing that continuum or gradation from Neanderthals to modern humans are at least 107 individuals from five sites who are usually grouped with fossils categorized as anatomically modern humans. However, since they are close to that subjective line which divides them from the Neanderthals, they are often described as "archaic moderns" or stated to have "Neanderthal affinities" or "Neanderthal features."

Creationists maintain that the differences found in the fossil material between Neanderthals and modern humans are the result of geography, not evolution. Of the 133 fossil individuals that are "close to the line" between Neanderthal and modern European morphology, all but four of them are from Eastern or Central Europe. If the differences between the Neanderthals and modern Europeans were ones reflecting a degree of geographic isolation, perhaps Eastern Europe is where the hybridization or the homogenization began.

If the fossils mentioned above could constitute a gradation within a single, genetically diverse, population, an obvious question is: "Why do evolutionists place them in two separate species?" The answer is that the theory of human evolution demands such separation. Humans are alleged to have evolved from the australopithecines—a group of extinct primates. In other words, we evolved from beings who were not only outside of our species, but were also outside of our genus. Hence, the evolutionist must create categories, species, or intermediate steps between the australopithecines and modern humans in an attempt to create an alleged evolutionary sequence. Fossils that are very similar are placed in one species. Fossils with some differences from the first group are placed in another species.

Evolutionists must create species, whether they are legitimate or not, in an attempt to show the stages or steps that they believe we passed through in our evolution from lower primates. Hence, most evolutionists today place the Neanderthals in a species separate from modern humans. Some evolutionists believe that the Neanderthals evolved into (some) modern humans. Others believe that the Neanderthals were a failed evolutionary experiment that did not quite make it to full humanity and became extinct. In either case, most evolutionists do not believe that the Neanderthals themselves were fully human, at least in a behavioral sense. The fossil evidence suggests otherwise. The full range of genetic and behavioral variation within the human family encompasses the Neanderthals.

Neanderthal burial practice

At least 475 Neanderthal fossil individuals have been discovered so far at about 124 sites in Europe, the Near East, and western Asia. This number includes those European archaic Homo sapiens fossils that are now called Neanderthal or pre-Neanderthal. Of these 475 Neanderthal individuals, at least 258 of them (54%) represent burials—all of them burials in caves or rock shelters.

Further, it is obvious that caves were used as family burial grounds or cemeteries, as numerous sites show.

The reason we have so many Neanderthal fossils is because they did bury their dead. (The bodies were thus protected from carnivore activity.) Most anthropologists recognize burial as a very human and a very religious act. Richard Klein (Stanford University) writes: "Neanderthal graves present the best case for Neanderthal spirituality or religion . . . ."[13] Only humans bury their dead.

Neanderthals and modern humans buried together

Perhaps the strongest evidence that Neanderthals were fully human and of our biblical "kind" is that at four sites people of Neanderthal morphology and people of modern human morphology were buried together. In all of life, few desires are stronger than the desire to be buried with one's own people. Skhul Cave, Mount Carmel, Israel, is considered to be a burial site of anatomically modern *Homo sapiens* individuals. Yet, Skhul IV and Skhul IX fossil skulls are closer to the Neanderthal configuration than they are to modern humans.[14] Qafzeh, Galilee, Israel, is also considered to be an anatomically modern burial site. However, Qafzeh skull 6 is clearly Neanderthal in its morphology.[15] Tabun Cave, Mount Carmel, Israel, is one of the classic Neanderthal burial sites. But the Tabun C2 mandible is more closely aligned with modern mandibles found elsewhere.[16] The Krapina Rock Shelter, Croatia, is one of the most studied Neanderthal burial sites. A minimum of 75 individuals are buried there. The remains are fragmentary making diagnosis difficult. However, the addition of several newly identified fragments to the Krapina A skull (now known as Krapina 1) reveals it to be much more modern than was previously thought, indicating that it is intermediate in morphology between Neanderthals and modern humans.[17]

That Neanderthals and anatomically modern humans were buried together constitutes strong evidence that they lived together, worked together, intermarried, and were accepted as members of the same family, clan, and community. The false distinction made by evolutionists today was not made by the ancients. To call the Neanderthals "Cave Men" is to give a false picture of who they were and why caves were significant in their lives. The human family is a unified family. "From one man He (God) made every nation of men, that they should inhabit the whole earth . . . " (Acts 17:26).

Neanderthal burial practice and the burial practice in Genesis

In comparing the Neanderthal burial practice with Genesis, I do not wish to imply that Abraham or his ancestors or his descendants were Neanderthals. What the relationship was—if any—between the people of Genesis and the Neanderthals we do not know. Young Earth Creationists tend to believe that the Neanderthals were a post-Flood people. What is striking is that the burial practice of the Neanderthals seems to be identical with that of the post-Flood people of Genesis.

Genesis 23:17–20 records a business transaction between Abraham and the Hittite, Ephron. Abraham wanted to purchase property in order to bury Sarah. We read:

> Afterward Abraham buried his wife Sarah in the cave in the field of Machpelah near Mamre (which is at Hebron) in the land of Canaan. So the field and the cave in it were deeded to Abraham by the Hittites as a burial site.

Upon his death (Genesis 25:7–11), Abraham was buried in that same cave. In Genesis 49:29–32, Jacob instructs his sons that he, too, is to be buried in that cave where Abraham and Sarah were buried. We then learn that Jacob buried his wife, Leah there, and that Isaac and Rebekah were buried there also. Abraham and Sarah, Isaac and Rebekah, and Jacob and Leah were all buried in the cave in the field of Machpelah which Genesis 23:20 states Abraham purchased "as a burial site." Only Sarah died in the geographic area of the cave. All of the others had to be transported some distance to be buried there, and Jacob's body had to be brought up from Egypt. It was important then, as it is today, to be buried with family and loved ones. Certainly, if the Neanderthal burial practice was similar to that of the people of Genesis, it suggests that the Neanderthals were very much like us. It is not without significance that both Lazarus and Jesus were buried in caves (John 11:38; Matthew 27:60), and that this practice has continued in many cultures up to modern times.

The archaeological evidence

The claim that the Neanderthals were culture-thin is surprising considering the evidence now available. The Neanderthals are alleged to be less than fully human because they had no glue or adhesives for hafting tools, no unequivocal art objects, no boats, canoes, or ships, no bows and arrows, no cave paintings, no domesticated animals or plants, no hooks, nets, or spears for fishing, no lamps, no metallurgy, no mortars and pestles, no musical instruments, no needles or awls for sewing, no ropes for carrying things, no sculpture, and no long distance overland trade.

The Indians of Tierra del Fuego, at the extreme southern tip of South America, were hunter-gatherers. They were considered to be among the most primitive people on earth. Ashley Montagu (Princeton University) writes that these Indians:

> [They] . . . live in perhaps the worst climate in the world, a climate of bitter cold, snow, and sleet, and heavy rains a great deal of the time, yet they usually remain entirely naked. During extremely cold weather they may wear a loose cape of fur and rub their bodies with grease.[18]

When Charles Darwin went on his famous around-the-world voyage, he visited the Fuegians. In his fascinating work, *The Voyage of the Beagle*, Darwin describes Fuegian life and culture.[22] It is difficult to compare people living in historic times with people we know only from fossils and cultural remains. Nevertheless, a strong case could be made that the cultural inventory of the Fuegians was less complex and extensive than was the cultural inventory of the Neanderthals. Yet, no one considered the Fuegians to be less than fully human, except Darwin, who believed that they were too primitive (sub-human) to be evangelized. Darwin was proven wrong by missionaries who did evangelize them. In fairness to Darwin, he later admitted his mistake regarding the spiritual potential of the Fuegians.[19]

One of the most brutal episodes in human history was the genocide of the full-blooded Tasmanians about a century ago. The genocide was allowed because evolutionists claimed that the Tasmanians were not fully human. The reason their full humanity was doubted was because evolutionists applied the false test of culture. Jared Diamond (University of California, Los Angeles) states in his article "Ten Thousand Years of Solitude" that any anthropologist would describe the Tasmanians as "the most primitive people still alive in recent centuries."[20] Of all of the people in the world, they were considered among the least technologically advanced. Hence, they were considered less evolved than other people.

Like the Indians of Tierra del Fuego, the cultural inventory of the Tasmanians, as described by Diamond, was less complex and extensive than was the cultural inventory of the Neanderthals. Yet, the Tasmanians proved that they were fully human. How did they prove it? They passed the fertility test. Although all full-blooded Tasmanians are gone, there are many Tasmanians of mixed blood today because in those early days many Caucasian men married Tasmanian women.

The following items suggest the full humanity of the Neanderthals.

Neanderthals as occupational hunters

The lifestyle of the Neanderthals can be summed up in just one word—hunting. To study the Neanderthal sites with their collections of the largest game animals gives the overwhelming impression that they were occupational hunters. Fossils of large animals are found in association with Neanderthal fossils at over half of the Neanderthal sites.

The evidence can be summarized as follows:

1. The largest group of animals found at Neanderthal sites are the very same types of animals used by humans for food today.

2. These animals are usually very large grazers, unlikely to be carried to the sites by carnivores.

3. Many show cut marks made by stone tools indicating that they were butchered.

4. The Neanderthals had the thrusting spears, hand axes, and other weapons to effectively hunt these animals.

5. The Neanderthal fossils show the injuries typical of those who handle large animals, such as cowboys.

Thus, it seems impossible to deny the Neanderthals the reputation they so richly deserve—stunning big game hunters.

Especially stunning is that about half of the Neanderthal sites that have fossil animal remains have fossils of elephants and woolly mammoths. Paleontologist Juan Luis Arsuaga writes:

> The elephant is the largest possible game animal on the face of the earth .... Beyond the physical capacity of prehistoric humans to hunt elephants, the crux of the polemic is in their mental capacity to develop and execute complex hunting strategies based on seasonally predictable conditions. Planning is powerful evidence for [the Neanderthals having fully human] consciousness.[21]

At Schöningen, Germany, were found three fir spears, fashioned like modern javelins, cleft at one end to accommodate stone points. They are the world's oldest throwing spears, dated by evolutionists at about 400,000 years old. They are six to seven and one-half feet long, and required powerful people to use them. It proves that there were big-game hunters at that time, and suggests a long tradition of hunting with such tools. It is presumed that the Neanderthals used them.[22] "If they are what they seem to be, these would be the first known weapons to incorporate two materials, in this case stone and wood. The Neanderthals almost surely used the many stone points found in Mousterian sites for the same purpose."[23] At the same site was found on a bed of black peat a fossilized horse pelvis with a wooden lance sticking out of it.[24]

Neanderthals and art

There is a problem in the recognition of evidence for "art" among the Neanderthals. The presence of art is considered a major indication of full humanity when dealing with fossil humans. Not only is other evidence regarding the full humanity of the Neanderthals not given proper weight, but the evidence for art among the Neanderthals has been seriously under-reported because of a subjective bias. The reason for this bias is an attempt to protect the field of paleoanthropology from the charge of racism.[25]

This under-reporting of art among the Neanderthals is confirmed by prehistorian Paul Bahn who writes regarding the attempts to make the Neanderthals a separate species:

> . . . in essence this boils down to stating that the Neanderthals were so different from ourselves that a firm line can be drawn between them and us, a view that is by no means universally held. To shore up this approach, all the growing body of evidence for "art" before 40,000 years ago is simply dismissed and ignored.[26]

Tools are found at most Neanderthal sites. Since they are not the artistic, delicate tools that are found in the Upper Stone Age, it has been assumed that the Neanderthals had not evolved mentally to the stage where they could make such tools. This criticism is absurd. The Neanderthal tools are what one would expect for a hunting people. Their tools are the utensils of the butcher shop, not the sterling silver utensils of a fancy French restaurant. Many archaeologists miss the point. It is not just a fancy tool that is a work of art, any tool is a work of artistic conceptualization.

Juan Luis Arsuaga states that making a stone tool is actually a work of art or sculpture. He writes: "Purposeful chipping at a stone is like sculpture in that it requires carefully chosen target points, very accurately aimed blows, a correctly calculated angle of impact, and well-regulated force."[27]

The story is told of a child who watched a sculptor take a large block of granite and over many weeks produced the statue of a man. Overcome with awe, the child asks the sculptor: "How did you know that man was in the rock?" The sculptor "knew" that the man was in the rock in the same way that the Neanderthals "knew" that the tools were in the stones. Both works are the product of a mind with conceptual ability. And the evidence shows that the Neanderthals had such ability.

The Neanderthals also had other works of art. A few of them include jewelry ornaments (bone, teeth, and ivory) with Neanderthal fossils[28] and iron pyrites with engraving. One site had a 15-inch-long piece of an elephant tibia with what appears to be engraving with seven lines going in one direction and twenty-one lines going in another direction. Two other pieces of bone have cut lines that seem to be too regular to be accidental. Archaeologist Dietrich Mania (University of Jena) says: "They are graphic symbols. To us it's evidence of abstract thinking and human language."[29]

In La Roche-Cotard, France, a stunning discovery of Neanderthal rock art is described as a human "face-mask" of palm-sized flint that has been reworked and altered. It was found in ice-age deposits. Its identification with the Neanderthals is based on its being "side by side with Mousterian tools"[30] in an undisturbed layer eight feet under the surface. The rock was hand-trimmed to enhance its human appearance by percussion flaking, the same way stone tools were made. Its human appearance was further enhanced "by a shard of animal bone pushed through a hole behind the bridge of the nose creating the appearance of eyes or eyelids." The report adds: "It is clearly not accidental since the bone is fixed firmly in place by two tiny wedges of flint . . . ."[31]

In addition, a flute made from the thighbone of a cave bear using the same seven-note system as is found in western music was discovered in a cave in Slovenia (northern Yugoslavia). It is associated with Mousterian tools.[32] Mousterian tools are normally the type made by Neanderthals.

Neanderthals and bone tools

Bone tools are considered to be more sophisticated than stone tools. It is not unusual to read anthropologists who claim that the Neanderthals were too primitive to have made bone tools. These anthropologists have not done their homework. Besides the mention of bone jewelry above, the scientific literature records bone tools at the following sites:

1. Bilzingsleben, Germany. This Neanderthal site has many hearths and has produced the world's largest collection of bone artifacts, with workshops for working bone, stone, and wood.[33]

2. Castel di Guido, Italy. At this Neanderthal site 5,800 bone and Acheulean stone artifacts were discovered. Some bone implements were rather simple. "Other bone implements show a higher degree of secondary flaking and are comparable to the classic forms of stone tools; especially remarkable are several bone bifaces made with bold, large flake removals. The

presence and abundance of undeniable, deliberately shaped bone tools make Castel di Guido a truly exceptional site."[34]

3. Fontana Ranuccio, Italy. This Neanderthal site contains some of the earliest artifacts found in Europe—Acheulean tools, including well-made hand axes, bone tools that were flaked, like stone, by percussion, and bifaces (hand axes) made of elephant bone.[35]

4. La Ferrassie Rock Shelter, France. The Neanderthal site contains tools that are of the Charentian Mousterian culture,[36] together with an engraved bone found with the La Ferrassie 1 fossil individual.

5. La Quina Rock Shelter, France. This Neanderthal site contains bone tools such as antler digging picks and highly modified lower ends of wild horse humeri.[37]

6. Petralona Cave, Greece. Evidence of the controlled use of fire is seen by blackened fire-stones and ashes. It would be impossible for fire in the cave to be of non-human origin. Artifacts at this Neanderthal site include stone tools of the early Mousterian culture and bone awls and scrapers.[38]

7. Régourdou Cave, France. This Neanderthal site contains bone tools, such as an antler digging pick and an awl.[39]

Neanderthals and space allocation

The ability to allocate specific areas for living, working, trash, and other purposes is considered to be a characteristic of a fully developed human mind. For some reason, this mental and conceptual ability by the Neanderthals has been questioned. The scientific literature shows that the Neanderthals clearly had this ability.

1. Arago Cave (Tautavel), France. Excavations show the presence of structured and walled living areas indicating cognitive and social capacity in Neanderthal populations.[40]

2. Arcy-sur-Cure caves, France. At this Neanderthal site there is evidence of a separation between ground that was littered with debris and clear ground, which suggests an original wall that separated the living area from the damp part of the cave, indicating the socially structured use of space.[41]

3. Bilzingsleben, Germany. The Neanderthal people here made structures similar to those made by Bushmen of southern Africa today. Three circular foundations of bone and stone have been uncovered, 9 to 13 feet across, with a long elephant tusk possibly used as a center post. A 27-foot-wide circle of pavement made of stone and bone may have been an area used for cultural activities with a anvil of quartzite set between the horns of a huge bison.[42]

4. La Chaise Caves, France. This Neanderthal site contains the presence of structured and walled living areas indicating cognitive and social capacity.[43]

5. La Ferrassie Rock Shelter, France. This Neanderthal site contains a rectangle of calcareous stones, 3 x 5 meters, carefully laid one beside the other to construct a flat surface for "clearly intentional work."[44]

6. Le Lazaret Cave, France. Richard Klein states that this Neanderthal site contains "clusters of artifacts, bones, and other debris that could mark hut bases or specialized activity areas." Klein adds, "The presence of a structure is suggested by an 11 x 3.5 m concentration of artifacts and fragmented animal bones bounded by a series of large rocks on one side and by the cave wall on the other. The area also contains two hearths . . . . The rocks could have supported poles over which skins were draped to pitch a tent against the wall of the cave."[45]

Neanderthals and technology

The Neanderthal site at Umm el Tlel, Syria, is dated at about 42,500 years of age.[46] The site contains Mousterian tools hafted with bitumen at very high temperatures. Prior to this, the earliest hafted tools were dated at about 10,000 years of age. The *Nature* report continues: "These new data suggest that Palaeolithic people had greater technical ability than previously thought, as they were able to use different materials to produce tools."[47] Simon Holdaway (La Trobe University, Australia) states: ". . . evidence for hafting in the Middle Palaeolithic may indicate that more complex multi-component forms existed earlier, so *changing our perceptions of the relationships between the two periods.*"[48] That is a remarkable statement. Just a few years ago, we were repeatedly told that the Neanderthals had no adhesives.

Conclusion

The evidence suggests that we need to rethink our attitude toward the Neanderthals. All that we could reasonably expect from the fossil and archaeological records supports the full humanity of the Neanderthals, our worthy ancestors.

7. See *New Scientist*, June 14, 2003. p. 50.

8. Donald Johanson and James Shreeve, *Lucy's Child* (New York: William Morrow & Company, 1989), 49.

9. See *Discover*, December 2006, p. 40.

10. *Science*, July 11, 1997, p. 177.

11. *Nature*, October 21, 1993, p. 700.

12. *Scientific American*, August 2003, p. 24.

13. *Science*, June 1, 2001, p. 1656.

14. *New Scientist*, May 17, 2003, p. 14.

15. *Proceedings of the National Academy of Science* 98(2), January 16, 2001, pp. 537–542.

16. *Cell* 90, July 11, 1997, pp. 19–30.

17. *Proceedings of the National Academy of Science* 98(2), January 16, 2001, pp. 537–542.

18. See *Bones of Contention*, pp. 178–179.

19. D. Johanson and J. Shreeve, *Lucy's Child* (New York: William Morrow and Company, 1989), p. 49.

20. Richard G. Klein, *The Human Career: Human Biological and Cultural Origins* (Chicago: The University of Chicago Press, 1989), 236–237.

21. Robert S. Corruccini, "Metrical Reconsideration of the Skhul IV and IX and Border Cave 1 Crania in the Context of Modern Human Origins," *American Journal of Physical Anthropology* 87:4 (April 1992): 433–445.

22. Ibid., 440–442.

23. R. M. Quam and F. H. Smith, "Reconsideration of the Tabun C2 'Neanderthal,'" *American Journal of Physical Anthropology* Supplement 22 (1996): 192.

24. N. Minugh-Purvis and J. Radovcic, "Krapina A: Neanderthal or Not?," *American Journal of Physical Anthropology* Supplement 12 (1991): 132.

25. Ashley Montagu, *Man: His First Two Million Years* (New York: Dell Publishing Co., Inc. 1969), 143–144.

26. Charles Darwin, *Voyage of the Beagle*, in the *Everyman's Library* series. (London: J. M. Dent & Sons, 1959) 194–219. Originally published in 1826, 1836, and 1839.

27. Jared Diamond, "Ten Thousand Years of Solitude," *Discover*, March 1993, 51.

28. Juan Luis Arsuaga, *The Neanderthal's Necklace* (New York: Four Walls Eight Windows, 2002), 273.

29. Hartmut Thieme, "Lower Palaeolithic hunting spears from Germany," *Nature* 385 (27 February 1987): 807–810.

30. Arsuaga, *The Neanderthal's Necklace*, 273.

31. Ibid., 182.

32. The details of this very real problem are beyond the scope of this chapter, but are fully explained in Section III of my book, *Bones of Contention*, Revised edition, available from Answers in Genesis.

33. Paul Bahn, "Better late than never," a review of *Timewalkers: The Prehistory of Global Colonization* by Clive Gamble, *Nature* 369 (16 June 1994): 531.

34. Arsuaga, *The Neanderthal's Necklace*, 32.

35. Jean-Jacques Hublin, Fred Spoor, Marc Braun, Frans Zonneveld, and Silvana Condemi, "A late Neanderthal associated with Upper Palaeolithic artifacts," *Nature* 381 (16 May 1996): 224–226. Paul G. Bahn, "Neanderthals emancipated," *Nature* 394 (20 August 1998): 719–721.

36. Rick Gore, "The First Europeans," *National Geographic*, July 1997, 110–111.

37. Avis Lang, "French School, 300th Century B. C." *Natural History*, March 2004, 23.

38. Douglas Palmer, "Neanderthal art alters the face of archaeology," *New Scientist*, 6 December 2003, 11.

39. Kate Wong, "Neanderthal Notes," *Scientific American*, September 1997, 28–30. "Early Music," *Science* 276 (11 April 1997): 205.

40. Rick Gore, "The First Europeans," *National Geographic,* July 1997, 110–111.

41. F. Mallegni and A. M. Radmilli, "Human Temporal Bone From the Lower Paleolithic Site of Castel di Guido, Near Rome, Italy," *American Journal of Physical Anthropology* 76:2 (June 1988): 177.

42. Klein, *The Human Career*, 344, 584.

43. Michael H. Day, *Guide to Fossil Man*, Fourth edition (Chicago: The University of Chicago Press, 1986), 39.

44. Brian Hayden, "The cultural capacities of Neanderthals: a review and re-evaluation," *Journal of Human Evolution* 24:2 (February 1993): 117.

45. Day, *Guide to Fossil Man*, 92.

46. Ibid., 120.

47. Hayden, "The cultural capacities of Neanderthals," 136.

48. Ibid, 123, 133.

49. Gore, "The First Europeans," 110–111.

50. Hayden, "The cultural capacities of Neandertals," 136.

51. Ibid., 117, 133.

52. Klein, *The Human Career*, 349–350.

53. Tim Folger and Shanti Menon, ". . . Or Much Like Us?" *Discover*, January 1997, 33.

54. Eric Boëda, Jacques Connan, Daniel Dessort, Sultan Muhesen, Norbert Mercier, Hélène Valladas, and Nadine Tisnérat, "Bitumen as a hafting material on Middle Palaeolithic artifacts," *Nature* 380 (28 March 1996): 336-338.

55. Simon Holdaway, "Tool hafting with a mastic," *Nature* 380 (28 March 1996): 288. Emphasis mine.

Marvin Lubenow has a Master of Theology degree (ThM) from Dallas Theological Seminary with a major in systematic theology, and a Master of Science degree (MS) from Eastern Michigan University with a major in anthropology. He is the author of *Bones of Contention*, the leading creationist book on so-called "apemen" fossils. Mr. Lubenow retired from the faculty of Christian Heritage College in 1995 where he was Professor of Bible and Apologetics.

Ida: The Missing Link?

by A. P. Galling

A new find was reported to the scientific community in May of 2009 and quickly rocketed to the heights of media hype as a team of scientists revealed "Ida," the latest and greatest supposed missing link. But does Ida actually support "the evolution of early primates, and, ultimately, modern human beings," as one news outlet reported?[1]

Another reporter raved, "The search for a direct connection between humans and the rest of the animal kingdom has taken 200 years—but it was presented to the world today at a special news conference in New York."[2]

Formally identified as *Darwinius masillae* (in honor of Charles

© Masr | Dreamstime.com

Darwin), the fossil originated in Germany and is purportedly 47 million years old. One scientist gave the find the nickname Ida (after his daughter).

Despite the hype, Ida looks nothing like a transitional "ape-man," instead looking quite like a modern lemur.

As for a more level-headed explanation of the evolutionary excitement, the *Wall Street Journal* reports:

Anthropologists have long believed that humans evolved from ancient ape-like ancestors. Some 50 million years ago, two ape-like groups walked the Earth. One is known as the tarsidae, a precursor of the tarsier, a tiny, large-eyed creature that lives in Asia. Another group is known as the adapidae, a precursor of today's lemurs in Madagascar.

Based on previously limited fossil evidence, one big debate had been whether the tarsidae or adapidae group gave rise to monkeys, apes, and humans. The latest discovery bolsters the less common position that our ancient ape-like ancestor was an adapid, the believed precursor of lemurs.[3]

Thus, rather than an apeman-like missing link that some media sources have irresponsibly implied, the real story is quite underwhelming and should in no way faze creationists. Let's first review the facts:

- The well-preserved fossil (95 percent complete, including fossilized fur and more) is about the size of a raccoon and includes a long tail. It resembles the skeleton of a lemur (a small, tailed, tree-climbing primate). The fossil does not resemble a human skeleton.

- The fossil was found in two parts by amateur fossil hunters in 1983. It eventually made its way through fossil dealers to the research team.

- Ida has opposable thumbs, which the ABC News article states are "similar to humans' and unlike those found on other modern mammals" (i.e., implying that opposable thumbs are evidence of evolution). Yet lemurs today have opposable thumbs (like all primates). Likewise, Ida has nails, as do other primates. And the talus bone is described as "the same shape as in humans," despite the fact that there are other differences in the ankle structure.[4]

- Unlike today's lemurs (as far as scientists know), Ida lacks the "grooming claw" and a "toothcomb" (a fused row of teeth) In fact, its teeth are more similar to a monkey's. These are minor differences easily explained by variation within a kind.

Given these facts, it may seem incredible that anyone would hail this find as a "missing link." Yet British naturalist David Attenborough claims:

> "Now people can say, 'Okay, you say we're primates . . . show us the link.' The link, they would have said until now, is missing. Well, it is no longer missing."[5]

Unbelievably, Attenborough claims his interpretation is "not a question of imagination."

The creationist interpretation

The principles that inform creationists about Ida are some of the same that allow creationists to interpret fossil after fossil hailed as "transitional forms":

1. **Nothing about this fossil suggests it is anything other than an extinct, lemur-like creature.** Its appearance is far from chimpanzee, let alone "apeman" or human.

2. **A fossil can never show evolution.** Fossils are unchanging records of dead organisms. Evolution is an alleged process of change in live organisms. Fossils show "evolution" only if one presupposes evolution, then uses that presupposed belief to *interpret* the fossil.

3. **Similarities can never show evolution.** If two organisms have similar structures, the only thing it *proves* is that the two have similar structures. One must presuppose evolution to say that the similarities are due to evolution rather than design. Furthermore, when it comes to "transitional forms," the slightest similarities often receive great attention while major differences are ignored.

4. **The remarkable preservation is a hallmark of rapid burial.** Team member Jørn Hurum of the University of Oslo said, "This fossil is so complete. Everything's there. It's unheard of in the primate record at all. You have to get to human burial to see something that's this complete." Even the contents of Ida's stomach were preserved. While the researchers believe Ida sunk to the bottom of a lake and was buried, this preservation is more consistent with a catastrophic flood.[6] Yet Ida was found with "hundreds of well-preserved specimens."[7]

5. **If evolution were true, there would be *real* transitional forms.** Instead, the best "missing links" evolutionists can come up with are strikingly similar to organisms we see today, usually with the exception of minor, controversial, and inferred anatomical differences.

6. **Evolutionists only open up about the lack of fossil missing links once a new one is found.** Sky News reports, "Researchers say proof of this transitional species finally confirms Charles Darwin's theory of evolution," while Attenborough commented that the missing link "is no longer missing."[8] So are they admitting the evidence was missing until now (supposedly)?

So it's clear what Ida is *not*. But just what is Ida? Because the fossil is similar to a modern lemur (a small, tailed, tree-climbing primate), it's unlikely that creationists need any interpretation of the "missing link" other than that it was a small, tailed, probably tree-climbing, and now extinct primate—from a kind created on Day 6 of Creation Week.

Much of the excitement over Ida appears to stem from a well-coordinated public relations effort to promote a documentary and a new book titled *The Link*. Filmmaker Atlantic Productions even launched a website to promote the discovery, revealingthelink.com.

Yet as Hurum commented, "This fossil will probably be the one that will be pictured in all textbooks for the next 100 years."[9] So while the media rush may at first have been a bid to promote the documentary and book, the ultimate result was one more trumped-up "missing link" presented to future generations as evidence of evolution.

It wasn't only creationists who disagreed with the "missing link" interpretation of Ida, however. In the article "Ida (*Darwinius masillae*): the Real Story of this 'Scientific Breakthrough'"[10], we quoted a slew of evolutionist scientists who felt that the Ida research was not necessarily inaccurate, but also may have been exaggerated because of financial motivations. The Associated Press reports, "A publicity blitz called [Ida] 'the link' that would reveal the earliest evolutionary roots of monkeys, apes and humans. Experts protested that Ida wasn't even a close relative."[11]

Of particular concern was that the "human ancestor" claims about Ida (which the media heavily hyped) had been cut from the peer-reviewed paper on the fossil. Further, it appeared the researchers had a vested interest in claiming Ida was significant, as they were trying to sell a book and promote a television documentary on the fossil. (Critics alleged that the team needed to earn a return on the fossil, which had been purchased at a high price).

Now, four scientists at U.S. universities have formalized some of the attacks on Ida's missing link status ("Convergent Evolution of Anthropoid-Like Adaptations in Eocene Adapiform Primates"[12]). The team, although evolutionists, agrees with our conclusion that Ida "belonged to a group more closely linked to lemurs than to monkeys, apes, or us," BBC News reports.[13]

The letter focuses on the description and analysis of a fossil called *Afradapis longicristatus*, which, the team argues, is closely related to Ida. Together, *A. longicristatus* and Ida (formally called *Darwinius masillae*) compose an extinct group of primates related to lemurs and lorises.

Research head Erik Seiffert, an anatomist/paleontologist at Stony Brook University, explained, "'The suggestion that Ida [was] . . . specifically related to the higher primates, namely monkeys apes and humans, was actually a minority view from the start. So it came as a surprise to many of us who are studying primate paleontology." Seiffert continued,

"We have analyzed a large data set based on observations we have made on almost 120 living and extinct primates and . . . we find . . . *Darwinius* and this new genus that we've described are not part of our ancestry. They are more closely related to lemurs and lorises than they are to tarsirs or monkeys, apes and humans. This study would effectively remove Ida from our ancestry."[14]

The University of Oslo's Jørn Hurum, who was on the original team investigating Ida, responded to Seiffert, *et al.*, in the *Nature* issue. "It's a very interesting paper, and—at last—this is the start of the scientific discussion around the specimen we described in May nicknamed Ida."

As far as we're concerned, the new study only reaffirms our appraisal of Ida: a (presumably extinct) lemur-like creature quite distinct from humans, neither suggesting evolution nor disproving creation in any way.

---

1.   Ned Potter, "Primate Fossil Could Be Key Link in Evolution," ABC News, May 19, 2009.

2.   Alex Watts, "Scientists Unveil Missing Link in Evolution," Sky News Online, May 19, 2009.

3.   http://online.wsj.com/article/SB124235632936122739.html.

4. J. L. Franzen et al., "Complete Primate Skeleton from the Middle Eocene of Messel in Germany: Morphology and Paleobiology," *PLoS One* 4 no. 5 (2009).

5. http://www.revealingthelink.com/the-implications.

6. Because of the location of this fossil, it may have been buried by a post-Flood period of residual catastrophism amid an unstable climate.

7. "Fossils from the Messel site," *The Guardian*, n.d.

8. http://news.sky.com/skynews/Home/World-News/Missing-Link-Scientists-In-New-York-Unveil-Fossil-Of-Lemur-Monkey-Hailed-As-Mans-Earliest-Ancestor/Article/200905315284582.

9. http://www.nydailynews.com/news/national/2009/05/19/2009-05-19_missing_link_found_fossil_of_47_millionyearold_primate_sheds_light_on_.html.

10. http://www.answersingenesis.org/articles/2009/05/21/ida-real-story.

11. http://www.cbsnews.com/stories/2009/10/22/tech/main5408922.shtml.

12. http://www.nature.com/nature/journal/v461/n7267/abs/nature08429.html.

13. http://news.bbc.co.uk/2/hi/science/nature/8318643.stm.

14. Ibid.

A. P. Galling earned his bachelor's degree in political science from Miami University in Oxford, Ohio. He writes regularly for the Answers in Genesis website and contributes to the weekly column "News to Note."

Meet "Ardi"

by A. P. Galling

Although first discovered in the early 1990s, the bones of *Ardipithecus ramidus* were only recently being nominated for evolutionists' fossil hall of fame—via a slew of papers in a special issue of the journal *Science* (October 2, 2009).[1] In it, Ardi's researchers describe the bones and make the case that Ardi is even more important in the history of human evolution than Lucy.

Despite claims of its evolutionary significance, one of the scientists who studied Ardi noted, "It's not a chimp. It's not a human."[2] That is, instead of looking like the hypothesized "missing link" (with both chimpanzee and human features), Ardi's anatomy—as reconstructed by the scientists—shows it to have been distinct from other apes as well as from humans. The researchers have consequently shunned the notion of a missing link: "It shows that the last common ancestor [between humans and] chimps didn't look like a chimp, or a human, or some funny thing in between," explained Penn State University paleontologist Alan Walker (who was not part of the study).[3]

The first question creationists have to answer is just what Ardi is. We can quickly eliminate important things that it isn't: it's not a human fossil, nor is it a complete fossil. In fact, even referring to "it" is deceptive, because Ardi is a partial skeleton put together based on a smattering of bones linked with at least 36 *A. ramidus* individuals. Dated at 4.4 million years old, the first bones were found in the early 1990s in Ethiopia. The delay in publishing an analysis was in part due to the poor state of the remains. "It took us many, many years to clean the bones in the National Museum of Ethiopia and then set about to restore this skeleton to its original dimensions and form; and then study it and compare it with all the other fossils that are known from Africa and elsewhere, as well as with the modern age," said the University of California–Berkeley's Tim White.[4]

But the *Evolution News & Views* blog offered a more critical look at how the poor state of the fossils casts doubt on the scientists' headline-grabbing claims. One telling quote comes from *National Geographic News* (in the same article that quoted Walker above):

> The first, fragmentary specimens of Ardipithecus were found at Aramis in 1992 and published in 1994. The skeleton announced today was discovered that same year and excavated with the bones of the other individuals over the next three field seasons. But it took 15 years before the research team could fully analyze and publish the skeleton, because the fossils were in such bad shape.
>
> After Ardi died, her remains apparently were trampled down into mud by hippos and other passing herbivores. Millions of years later, erosion brought the badly crushed and distorted bones back to the surface.
>
> They were so fragile they would turn to dust at a touch. To save the precious fragments, White and colleagues removed the fossils along with their surrounding rock. Then, in a lab in [Ethiopia], the researchers carefully tweaked out the bones from the rocky matrix using a needle under a microscope, proceeding "millimeter by submillimeter," as the team puts it in *Science*. This process alone took several years.
>
> Pieces of the crushed skull were then CT-scanned and digitally fit back together by Gen Suwa, a paleoanthropologist at the University of Tokyo.[3]

Thus, as a starting point, creationists should remember that—as with many fossils—the state of preservation is far less perfect than what media images and "reconstructions" portray. (The "complete," 4 feet [1.5 m] tall Ardi fossil, as reassembled, is shown on the cover of the special *Science* issue.)

We also know, as Walker explained (above), that Ardi actually shows many differences from both other apes and humans. Kent State University's Owen Lovejoy described some of the features: "She has opposable great toes and she has a pelvis that allows her to negotiate tree branches rather well. So half of her life is spent in the trees; she would have nested in trees and occasionally fed in trees, but when she was on the ground she walked upright pretty close to how you and I walk."[4] Obviously, we would point out that the scientists haven't actually observed Ardi walking; their assertion is based on their reconstruction of the bones. Furthermore, Ardi's feet not only had opposable big toes, but also lacked arches, which separates Ardi from humans and means "she could not walk or run for long distances," BBC News reports.[4] And *National Geographic News* notes, "Ardi would have walked on her palms as she moved about in the trees—more like some primitive fossil apes than like chimps and gorillas."[3]

In fact, despite the headlines and hype, the evolutionary researchers aren't even confident enough to say that Ardi is a human ancestor as opposed to simply an extinct ape. BBC News reports: "Even if it is not on the direct line to us, it offers new insights into how we evolved from the common ancestor we share with chimps, the team says."[4]

Asked whether *A. ramidus* was our direct ancestor or not, the team said more fossils from different places and time periods were needed to answer the question.

"We will need many more fossil recoveries from the period of 3–5 million years ago to confidently answer that question in the future," the scientists said in a briefing document that accompanied their journal papers.[4]

"But if Ardipithecus ramidus was not actually the species directly ancestral to us, she must have been closely related to it, and would have been similar in appearance and adaptation."

Not only does that uncertainty exist; several scientists have admitted skepticism over the Ardi reports. Harvard University paleoanthropologist David Pilbeam told ScienceNOW, "I find it hard to believe that the numerous similarities of chimps and gorillas evolved convergently."[5] (We, too, have criticized the idea of convergent evolution in the past—albeit from the opposite angle.)

Also, anatomist William Jungers of Stony Brook University criticizes the conclusion that Ardi could walk upright: "This is a fascinating skeleton, but based on what they present, the evidence for bipedality is limited at best. Divergent big toes are associated with grasping, and this has one of the most divergent big toes you can imagine. Why would an animal fully adapted to support its weight on its forelimbs in the trees elect to walk bipedally on the ground?" he told *National Geographic News*.[3]

Finally, some scientists have asked how Ardi fits into the evolutionary scheme with Australopithecines like Lucy, another supposed human ancestor said to have lived more recently than Ardi. Was there enough time, in the evolutionary timetable, for primitive Ardi to have evolved into less-primitive Lucy? The BBC quotes Chris Stringer of London's Natural History Museum, who said, "With Australopithecus starting from four million years ago, one would have thought that things would have moved further down the line by 4.4 million years ago. OK, you can have very rapid change, perhaps; or *Ardipithecus* might be a residual form, a relic of a somewhat older stage of evolution that had carried on. Perhaps we will find something more like Australopithecus at 4.4 million years old somewhere else in Africa."[4]

We must admit that from our perspective, we're growing desensitized to the fervor that increasingly surrounds each new fossil discovery claimed to support evolution. Surrounding Ardi's unveiling was a spectacular media frenzy, but in many ways it's little different than the hype over Ida less than five months earlier. That hype was quickly revealed to be unmerited at best and dishonest at worst. In the same way, the concerted release of so many papers on Ardi and the corresponding hubbub seems to perhaps have been more about attention-seeking than about science. Could it be that the ongoing pressure for scientists to find something of evolutionary "significance" has led to a systematic incentive to make a huge deal (to use the vernacular) out of otherwise trivial fossils?

Perhaps we're being a bit too rough, though. Evolutionists believe our own origins lie buried in such fossils as Ardi, so it's no wonder they have a desire to interpret such finds in the light of human evolution. But in the case of Ardi (and Ida, Lucy, etc.), good science abstains from making such untestable, presupposition-driven claims.

Given the number and scope of the papers presented on Ardi, it will take some time before creationists are confident in our conclusions on Ardi and her kin. Based on our first look, however, the facts seem solidly behind the idea that Ardi was a quadrupedal ape with relatively little in common with humans (i.e., no more than most apes); the key basis for the alleged Ardi–human link (which even the authors are hesitant to confirm) is the idea that it walked upright—an idea that even evolutionists have criticized. And we can't forget that all of these conclusions are inferred from digital reconstructions and fallible reconstructions of bones that were in very bad shape.

Without having a live "Ardi" to observe, scientists will only ever be able to come to probabilistic conclusions about its characteristics. As far as we're concerned, the evolutionary "threat" to creationists from Ardi is no more than that posed by Ida: viz., none.

1. You can read all eleven papers at http://www.sciencemag.org/ardipithecus.

2. http://news.discovery.com/archaeology/ardi-human-ancestor.html.

3. http://news.nationalgeographic.com/news/2009/10/091001-oldest-human-skeleton-ardi-missing-link-chimps-ardipithecus-ramidus.html.

4. http://news.bbc.co.uk/2/hi/8285180.stm.

5. http://news.sciencemag.org/sciencenow/2009/10/01-01.Html.

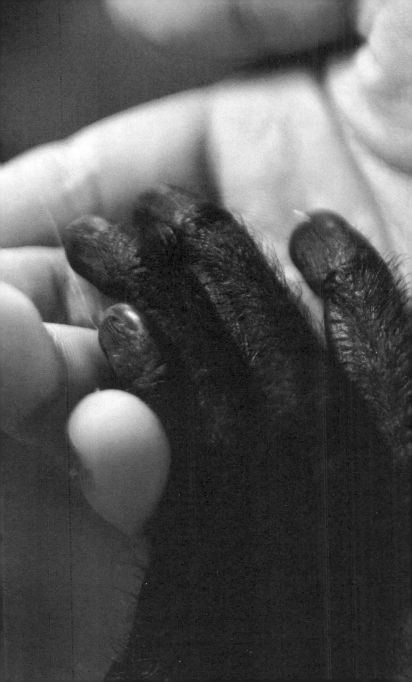

Apeman or Adam?

If you stop and think about where humans came from, there are really only two options, unless you allow for alien explanations. Man is either the product of billions of years of unguided evolutionary processes or the special creation of the Creator. Secular scientists today believe that man has no special place in the universe or the planet—we are just cosmic accidents. If this is true, the concept of morality has no foundation. This is not to say that these scientists are immoral, but that they have no ultimate standard they can use in describing morality.

If you are consistent in your thinking, what you believe about the past influences your actions—ideas have consequences. If you are a descendant of an ape then there is no such thing as an absolute truth with respect to morality. One person's opinion is just as valid as another's. If you are a descendant of Adam then you are a special creation of the Creator described in the Bible. If God made you, then you owe Him your devotion and find morality described in His words recorded in the Bible.

The Bible makes it clear that all mankind has fallen short of honoring God with their thoughts, words, and deeds (Romans 3:23). A quick look at God's standard for morality can help you see how far short you fall. Have you ever used God's name in a loose way (blasphemy)? Told a lie or deceived someone? Taken things that don't belong to you or desired things that belong to others (coveting)? The list continues, but you can probably already see that if God judged you by His moral standard, you would be guilty of countless sins before Him.

As a just God (Psalm 7:11), He must punish sin. Since this sin is against an infinitely holy God, the punishment itself is eternal. As a gracious God, He has provided a substitute for the payment of your sins against Him. Jesus Christ came as God in the flesh (John 1:1–14), lived a sinless life, and died on a cross taking God's wrath for sin upon Himself. Those who will repent of (turn from and abandon) their sins and place their full trust in Christ can be granted a pardon for their sin and a new life in Christ.

Please consider these truths and read the Gospel of John. This book of the Bible explains who Jesus was and what he has done for mankind. You are more than a highly-evolved ape— you are created in the image of God.